Business communications ar sk

Michael Fardon
Jo Osborne

Published by Osborne Books Limited
Unit 1B Everoak Estate
Bromyard Road, Worcester WR2 5HP
Tel 01905 748071
Email books@osbornebooks.co.uk
Website www.osbornebooks.co.uk

Design by Laura Ingham

Printed by CPI Group (UK) Limited, Croydon, CR0 4YY, on environmentally friendly, acid-free paper from managed forests.

British Library Cataloguing in Publication Data
A catalogue record for this book is available from the British Library

ISBN 978 1909173 538

Contents

Acknowledgements

The publisher wishes to thank the following for their help with the editing, reading and production of the book: Maz Loton, Bee Pugh and Cathy Turner. Thanks are also due to Laura Ingham for her designs for this series.

The publisher is indebted to the Association of Accounting Technicians for its help and advice to our authors and editors during the preparation of this text and to Getty Images for the reproduction of photographs on page 67.

Authors

Michael Fardon has extensive teaching experience of a wide range of banking, business and accountancy courses at Worcester College of Technology. He now specialises in writing business and financial texts and is General Editor at Osborne Books. He is also an educational consultant and has worked extensively in the areas of vocational business curriculum development.

Jo Osborne qualified as a Chartered Accountant with Ernst & Young in their London office. She then moved to Cable & Wireless where she spent two years in their internal audit department before moving into an investment appraisal role. Jo has taught AAT at Hillingdon College and until recently at Worcester College of Technology where she took on the role of AAT Coordinator.

Introduction

what this book covers

This book has been written specifically to cover the Unit 'Applied business communications and personal skills' which is mandatory for the AAT Level 2 Diploma in Accounting and Business.

The book contains a clear text with illustrative examples and case studies, chapter summaries and key terms to help with revision. Each chapter has a wide range of student activities, many based on the style of the AAT assessment.

relationship with Work Effectively in Accounting and Finance (WKAF)

The AAT's Level 2 Unit 'Work Effectively in Accounting and Finance (WKAF)', which forms part of the Level 2 Diploma, has certain elements in common with 'Applied business communications and personal skills (ABPS)'. The AAT states in its Study and Assessment Guide to ABPS:

> 'ABPS is about students evaluating their own communication and personal skills and recognising the importance of these skills in the business environment. The unit complements WKAF (Work Effectively in Accounting and Finance) which focuses on an accounting environment.'

This book acknowledges this overlap by presenting the common topics in a new and different way, relating its scenarios and activities to business contexts and situations rather than focusing solely on an accounting environment. The text therefore usefully complements the WKAF text by widening the student's appreciation of the business world. It also expands the development of students' skills by concentrating on the personal skills required in a business environment.

1 Communication skills at work

this chapter covers...

This chapter is an introduction to the 'Applied business communications and personal skills' Unit – it explains how all the parts of the Unit fit together. It then goes on to introduce all the different forms of business communication that you will need to know about and practise.

The main topics covered in this chapter are:

- *developing your skills in this Unit*
- *the ways in which businesses communicate with other businesses and the public*
- *how people working in business communicate between themselves*
- *the different methods of communication used by businesses, for example emails, letters, the telephone and discussions in meetings*
- *understanding that private communications and business communications can be very different in style as well as in content*
- *knowing that someone working in a business must give a good impression of that business by being polite and helpful to other businesses and the public by using business etiquette*

Lastly – remember that this chapter is an introduction to communication skills. Much of its content will be explained in more detail in the four chapters that follow. These chapters cover emails, letters, using telephones and holding meetings.

SOME NOTES ON 'SKILLS'

defining skills

This Unit is called 'Applied business communications and personal skills'. It is about developing your skills so that you will be better equipped to get a job and progress your working career.

What is a skill? A search on the Web might come up with something along the lines of the following:

a skill is the ability to do something well –

which comes naturally to you

or . . . which is a result of your own hard work

or . . . which is a result of special training

You can see from this that skills in the widest sense can include the skills that come naturally: eg the ability to run, sing, dance and speak in front of an audience. But there are also the skills that you can achieve through study (as in this Unit): bookkeeping, payroll, spreadsheets and learning how to study.

developing skills

This book is all about **developing** your **skills** – in other words expanding and improving them. It will be up to you to assess your abilities and:

- identify a range of skills which you find are easy to do and develop
- identify a range of skills which need working on and studying so that you can improve and develop them

When you have identified the skills that are easy to develop and those that are difficult, you can then plan a programme for improvement. You will have to monitor and adjust your programme regularly just as an athlete or gym member will plan a fitness programme which changes over time.

This process is illustrated in the diagram below.

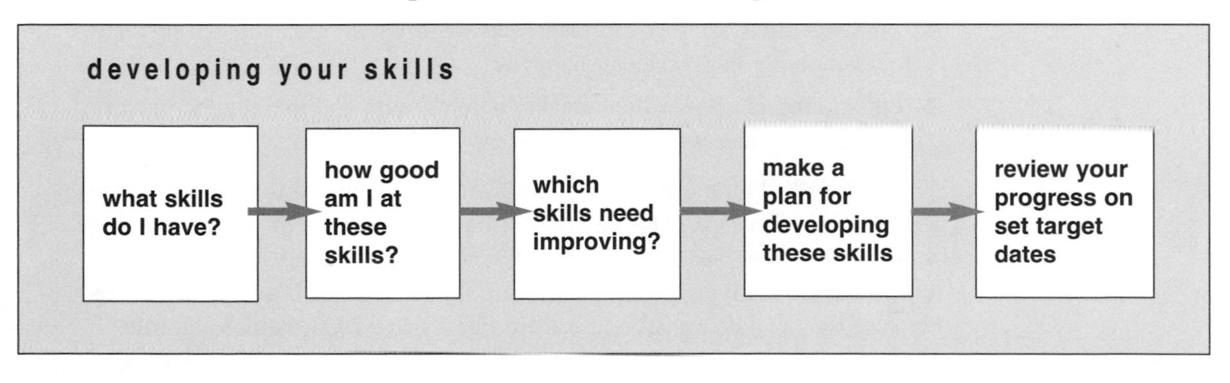

There are two main areas of skills which you will learn about and develop in this AAT Unit: **communication skills** and **personal skills**.

communication skills

These skills enable you to communicate in writing or by word of mouth with:

- work colleagues and managers
- people that an employer deals with, eg customers and other businesses

Communication skills are also commonly used **socially** with family and friends but normally in a much more informal way.

Business communications include:

- emails
- letters
- phone calls
- meetings

As you will see when studying this chapter, there are significant differences between business communications and day-to-day personal and social communications with family and friends.

personal skills

These are a different type of skills which are far more general and relate to:

- your personality
- your ability to deal with people, situations and problems

Personal skills – which will be described in more detail later in Chapter 6 of this book – include:

- **managing time**, which involves planning ahead and dealing with unexpected events
- **initiative**, which means 'seeing what needs to be done and then getting on and doing it'
- **commitment**, which means 'doing what it takes' and showing loyalty to people and organisations
- **perseverance**, a rather old-fashioned word which means 'sticking at it' or 'keeping going whatever happens'
- **embracing change**, which means 'dealing with and making the most of change', in other words, seeing change as a challenge rather than a threat

You can see that all these personal skills are not specific skills, such as being able to deal with spreadsheets, but will be very valuable to people working in an organisation such as a business. They can also be useful if they are applied to the studying process. They are also known as **transferable skills** because they can be transferred for use in a variety of situations and roles.

The diagram below illustrates how personal skills work.

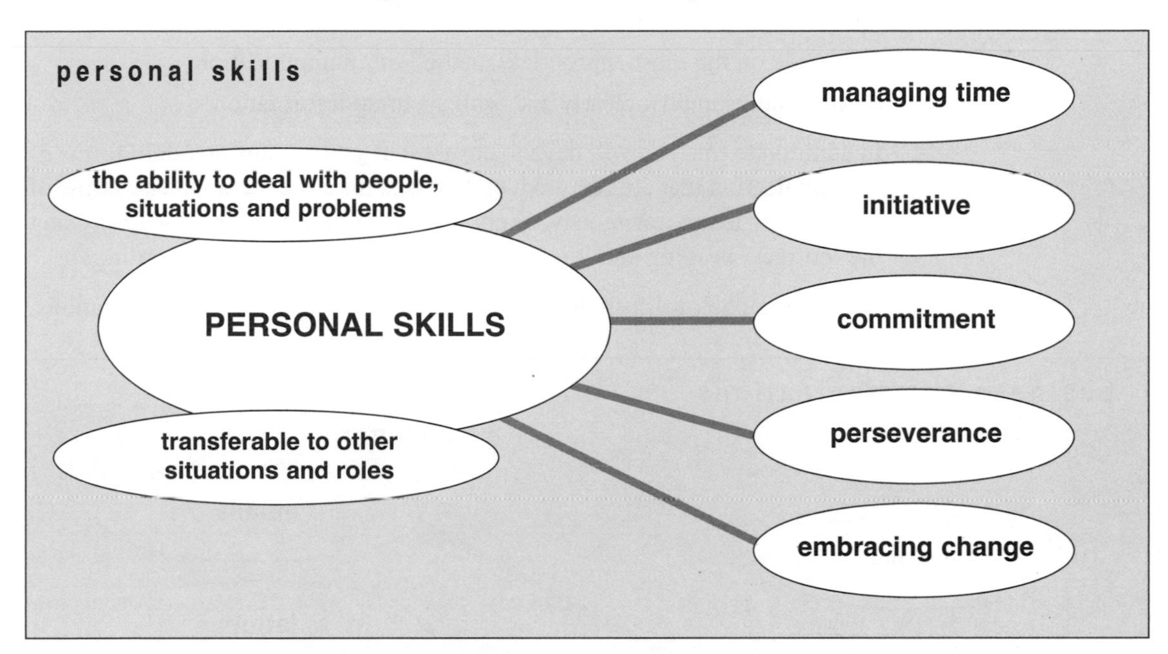

BUSINESS COMMUNICATIONS

ways of communicating

There are various ways of communicating at work and it is important to choose the right method for each situation. For example, an email may be appropriate to check the time of a meeting that you need to attend but is probably not the right way to communicate a notice of resignation.

Communication can either be within the organisation in which you work, or it can be with outsiders. These two types of communication are described as follows:

- **internal communication** – this could be with managers, colleagues in your own department, or with staff in other departments
- **external communication** – this could be with suppliers, customers, banks, delivery drivers or anyone who is external to the business you work for

When you are communicating with colleagues and managers that work **in the same organisation** as you it is important that you make sure that:

- you use the right method of communication
- you are polite - regardless of whether they are polite to you or not
- you reply to requests promptly and clearly

Similarly, if you need to communicate with people **outside the business** you must:

- decide on the most appropriate method of communication
- respond promptly, clearly and with accurate information

In addition to this you will have to ensure that you use any standard forms of communication that are required, eg letters setting out a company's terms of sale, chaser letters for money owed; often there are legal reasons for using the 'correct' wording and it is important that you stick to that wording.

The diagram below illustrates the main features of business communications.

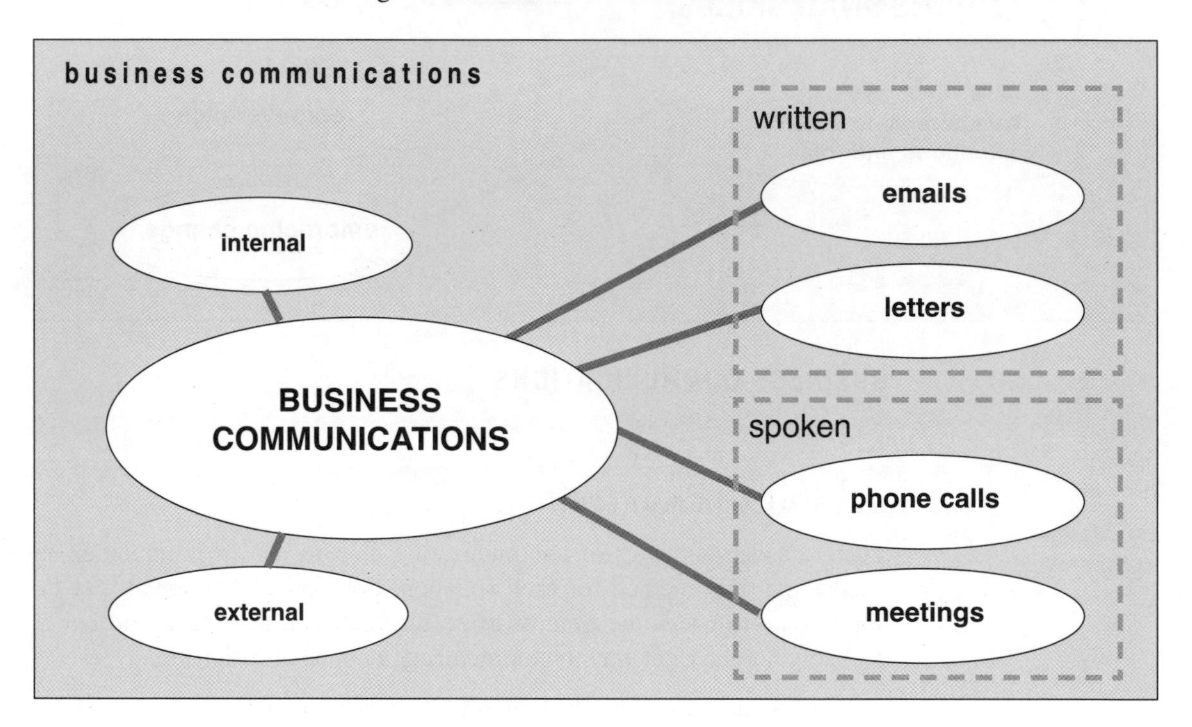

BUSINESS ETIQUETTE

You must also take a professional approach to communicating – this is known as '**business etiquette**'.

what is business etiquette?

With the growth of social media such as Facebook and Twitter and the 'language' which they use, it is easy to forget that there are certain standards that should be maintained when you are communicating in a work situation. It is important that employees follow appropriate **business etiquette**. This can be defined as:

'The behaviour that is expected in the workplace – it involves treating colleagues and outsiders that come into contact with the business with an equal degree of respect and courtesy.'

Note that business etiquette relates not only to your own workplace but also to dealings with other businesses and your customers.

We will deal with specific examples of business etiquette in the four chapters that follow this one. They deal in turn with emails, letters, telephone calls and meetings. It is important, however, to know about the basic principles which underlie business etiquette.

etiquette in personal relationships

You communicate meaningfully in personal relationships – for example with a partner, a best friend, or a family member – because you know them well. You phone, text, email, post on Facebook, meet up and stay in contact with them because you want to stay connected and you value the relationship.

etiquette in business relationships

Etiquette in business relationships is based on the same principles. The only significant difference is that you communicate with business contacts but you are not normally close buddies with them or married to them. But the relationship will still need to be **positive** and **respectful**, for example if you are selling a TV or answering the phone in a customer services department.

Look at the impression given by the two shop assistants shown below. It is not difficult to see which one is employing better business etiquette.

differences in language

The language used in personal relationships, however, is normally much more casual and familiar. Texting is commonly abbrevi8ed and this practice has spread to emailing. This language should never be used in business communications as it will seem over-familiar, inappropriate and even misleading. For example, the abbreviation 'lol' traditionally means 'laugh out loud' but is sometimes mistranslated as 'lots of love' which could cause all sorts of problems if you email this to a colleague or a customer.

some tips on good practice in business etiquette

If you are making face-to-face contact, for example selling something to a customer, meeting someone from another business, or meeting someone from the same business, you are establishing personal contact and need to:

- be polite and respectful
- give eye contact - but do not overdo it!
- listen carefully
- show appreciation of what is being said
- provide clear and accurate information
- follow up on anything that needs to be followed up

These, of course, are also the basic principles of 'customer care' which are so important in business.

some tips on business communications

In any form of communication between businesses and within a business you should also:

- use the type of language appropriate to the form of communication
- answer messages and confirm requests in a way that is appropriate to the form of communication – if you do not, the other person may think either that you have not received the message or are not that bothered about it
- tell people who try and contact you if you are going to be away from work
- remember that you are representing your business and should promote a positive image

In short, business etiquette is based on respect for others. For the individual it will improve employability and promotion prospects, for the business it will help to secure its reputation and success.

Now read the Case Study that follows. It includes examples of good business etiquette and poor business etiquette.

Case Study

ROBINO'S FAST FOOD – A FLY IN A BURGER

situation

Luke is employed as an assistant in the Customer Services Department of Robino's, a large chain of fast food restaurants. The following incident happened during September.

Thursday 5 September, 3.15pm

Luke receives the following email:

To: customerservices@robinos.com
From : marinablake@redcomms.com
Date: 5/09/20XX

Subject: Fly on my burger

Dear Sir/Madam,

Yesterday I purchased a burger from your Clapham restaurant and when I opened the packaging there was a dead fly stuck on the bun. I have taken a photograph and have attached it to this email. It was lucky that I saw the fly before I started to eat the burger.

I will be grateful if you would acknowledge my email and let me know what you propose to do about this situation.

I look forward to hearing from you soon.

Yours faithfully,

Mrs M. Blake

09942 993124

As Luke is going away for a long weekend that evening he decides to ignore the email and puts it on his 'to do' list to deal with when he returns to the office on Tuesday.

Tuesday 10 September 9.30am

Luke opens his emails and discovers a further email from Marina Blake:

To: customerservices@robinos.com
From : marinablake@redcomms.com
Date: 9/09/20XX

Subject: Fly on my burger

Dear Sir/Madam,

I am very disappointed that I have not heard from you regarding the email I sent you on Thursday. I intend to raise this matter with someone more senior in your organisation and may consider contacting the local newspaper.

I look forward to hearing from you soon.

Kind regards

Mrs M. Blake
09942 993124

Luke decides to telephone the customer straightaway and leaves the following voicemail message:

'Hi Marina, this is Luke from the Customer Services team at Robino's Restaurant in Clapham.

Sorry I didn't email back on Thursday but I was off on holiday that evening and ran out of time! I'm really sorry to hear about the fly on your burger – it must have been a real shock.

Mind you, you get what you pay for and the quality of the stuff we use in our burgers isn't great.

Anyway, email me your address and I'll try and send a voucher for a free burger or something in the post! Cheers!'

Luke thinks that he has dealt with the situation in an appropriate business-like manner.

question

What issues does this situation raise with regard to Luke's business etiquette?

solution

Business etiquette is based on respect for others. In this situation Luke has not shown respect for Mrs Blake.

This is what Luke should have done if he had used the correct business etiquette:

- Luke should have responded to the email when he received it on the Thursday, confirming that he had received it and politely explaining that he would investigate the matter and update Mrs Blake early the following week when he was back in the office.
- Luke should have used more appropriate business language in the phone message he left. Both the emails sent by Marina Blake have been signed Mrs M. Blake. In his message Luke should have called her Mrs Blake rather than Marina. Also he should not have finished the call with 'Cheers!' as this is too familiar. It would have been more appropriate to tell Mrs Blake that he would send her an email to confirm what he had said.
- Saying that he did not reply to her first email because he ran out of time before his holiday makes it look like he does not really care about the customer's problem with the fly.
- The phrase 'you get what you pay for and the quality of the stuff we use in our burgers isn't great,' does not promote a positive image of Robino's Restaurants.
- In his message Luke has ignored Mrs Blake's comment that she might contact the local newspaper. He should have mentioned this in his message to acknowledge how seriously he is taking the issue.
- Offering to send a voucher for 'a free burger or something' is not sufficient compensation for Mrs Blake. Luke should have said how seriously Robino's takes matters like this and that he would raise it with someone more senor in the business who would be in touch with her to arrange appropriate compensation.

Chapter Summary

- Some skills come easily to you when you have a natural aptitude for them; these are often physical skills such as being a good tennis player but can also include an aptitude for dealing with figures or for speaking in public.
- Other skills have to be studied and worked at, for example double-entry bookkeeping and writing letters.
- You need to assess your skills so that you can plan out how you can develop, improve and review them over a period of time.
- Communication skills, which include the ability to communicate by word of mouth or in writing, are important skills for working in business.
- Personal skills are an important development of your personality and enable you to deal with people, situations and problems. They are therefore also important skills for working in business.
- The main personal skills include: time management, initiative, commitment, perseverance and the ability to make the most of change. These skills are defined further in the Key Terms on the next page and explained in more detail in Chapter 6.
- Business communications can be internal or external and it is important to be able to choose the right kind of communication for each situation.
- Business etiquette is a positive form of respect and courtesy which you should always show both to colleagues and also to people outside your workplace.
- The language used in business communications is very different from the informal language used in texting and personal emails. It is part of business etiquette to use language that is respectful and clear in its meaning.

Key Terms

a skill	the ability to do something well; it may come naturally, it may need to be worked on
communication skills	skills needed to communicate, either in writing or by word of mouth
internal communication	communication within one organisation
external communication	communication with organisations or people outside your own organisation
personal skills	skills that relate to your personality and which enable you to deal with people and problems
managing time	planning ahead, dealing with unexpected events and meeting deadlines
initiative	seeing what needs to be done and then getting on and doing it
commitment	doing what it takes and showing loyalty
perseverance	keeping going whatever happens
embracing change	seeing change as a challenge rather than a threat
transferable skills	skills that can be used in a variety of situations and roles
business etiquette	when working in business, treating colleagues and outsiders with an equal degree of respect and courtesy

Activities

1.1 Decide which one or more of the following statements are correct about a skill. Tick the appropriate box or boxes in the table below.

1 doing something well that comes naturally to you

2 doing something well as a result of your own hard work

3 doing something well as a result of special training

	✔
(a) 1 only	
(b) 1 and 2	
(c) 2 and 3	
(d) 1, 2 and 3	

1.2 Write down in the numbered table below the following stages of skills development in the order in which they should be done.

- decide which skills need improving
- decide how good you are at these skills
- review your progress on set target dates
- identify the skills that you have
- make a plan for developing your skills

1
2
3
4
5

1.3 Decide which of the following are often used for business communications. Tick all that apply.

	✔
(a) Emails	
(b) Instagram	
(c) Texts	
(d) Letters	
(e) Facebook	
(f) Meetings	
(g) Telephone calls	
(h) Twitter	

1.4 Complete the following sentences by selecting the correct word from these two options:

personal **communication**

(a) '...................................... skills enable you to exchange information with work colleagues and other people external to the business by word of mouth or in writing.'

(b) '...................................... skills relate to your ability to deal with people, situations and problems and will reflect your personality.'

1.5 Match each of the personal skills listed below on the left with the correct definition on the right.

managing time	dealing with and making the most of change by seeing it as a challenge rather than a threat
initiative	seeing what needs to be done and then getting on and doing it
commitment	planning ahead, dealing with unexpected events and meeting deadlines
perseverance	doing what it takes and showing loyalty to people and organisations
embracing change	sticking at what you have to do and keeping going whatever happens

1.6 For each of the communications listed below decide whether it is an example of **internal** communication or **external** communication. Tick the appropriate column on the right.

	internal ✔	**external** ✔
A letter sent to a customer explaining that a delivery has been delayed		
An email sent to members of the customer services team arranging a team meeting for the following day		
A directors' meeting with the business's bank manager		
A telephone call between the sales manager and the customer services supervisor		
A telephone call between an accounts assistant and a supplier		
A marketing email to all customers currently on the business's database		

1.7 Read through the following situation and then answer the question below. The answer should be written down by individual students and could then form the basis of a class discussion.

situation

Martha is employed in the Customer Services Department of Redbag Ltd, a company that makes plastic carrier bags. She answers a call from a customer and the conversation goes as follows:

Martha: *'Good afternoon Redbag, can you hold please?'*

Martha then puts the caller on hold while she goes to fetch her coffee. She then takes the caller off hold.

Martha: *'Right, what did you say your name was?'*

Caller: *'This is Jeff Cummings, I'm the Sales Director at Georgina Clothing. I want to speak to you about.....'*

Martha interrupts:

'Hiya Jeff, how are you? I love Georgina Clothing, especially when I'm looking for something special for a night out. What can I do for you?'

Caller: *'I want to find out when we can expect our delivery of carrier bags, they were due here three days ago.'*

Martha: *'Hold on a sec, Jeff, I'll see what I can find out.'*

Martha does not put Jeff on hold but places the phone receiver on the desk and shouts across the office to the warehouse manager who is passing through the office:

'Mike, I've got some bloke from Georgina Clothing on the phone asking where his delivery is. Shall I tell him you'll call him back?'

Mike nods his head as if to say 'yes'. Martha picks up the phone but the caller has hung up.

You are to identify at least three examples of where Martha has failed to use business etiquette and suggest how she should have dealt with the situation in line with business etiquette.

Example of poor business etiquette	Suggested improvement

2 Business emails

this chapter covers...

This chapter explains what is needed to write a good business email. The first area it covers involves the structure of an email and the various elements it contains, including:

- *using the correct email address*
- *the reply function*
- *copying in other recipients using Cc (Carbon copy) and Bcc (Blind carbon copy)*
- *creating the appropriate wording for the subject line*
- *sending attachments*
- *adding security and passwords*

The second area the chapter covers is the actual writing of the email:

- *using an appropriate style for the text*
- *the 'dos' and 'don'ts' of email writing*
- *how to address the recipient using an appropriate salutation, for example 'Hi' or 'Dear Mr . . .'*
- *how to sign off an email using an appropriate complimentary close, for example 'Regards' or 'Best wishes'*

EMAILS – GOOD PRACTICE

business emails

Emails have now become one of the main ways in which people communicate, and businesses are no exception to this. Emails are used both internally to communicate with colleagues, and also externally to communicate with people and organisations outside the business. But what makes a good email and what sort of things should you try to avoid when you are writing an email?

Set out below is an example of a business email. Study the way in which it is set out and then read the points that follow.

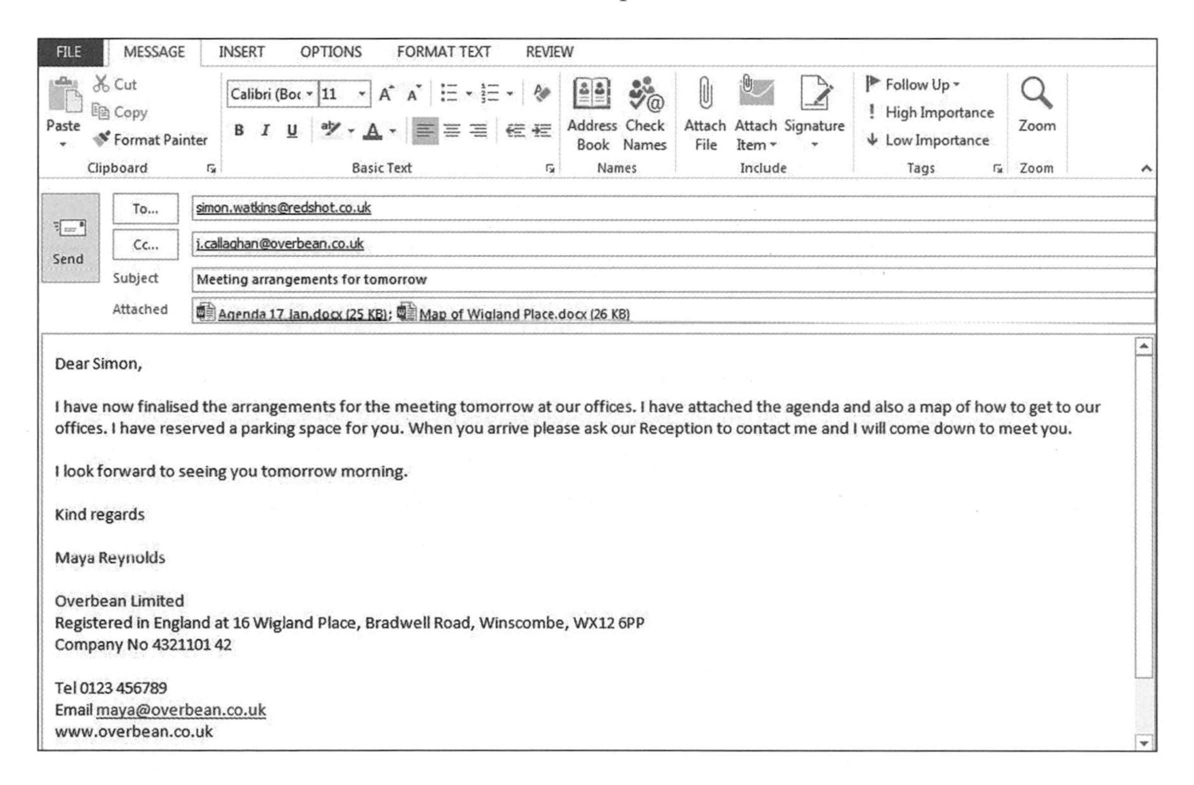

To... simon.watkins@redshot.co.uk
Cc... j.callaghan@overbean.co.uk
Subject Meeting arrangements for tomorrow
Attached Agenda 17 Jan.docx (25 KB); Map of Wigland Place.docx (26 KB)

Dear Simon,

I have now finalised the arrangements for the meeting tomorrow at our offices. I have attached the agenda and also a map of how to get to our offices. I have reserved a parking space for you. When you arrive please ask our Reception to contact me and I will come down to meet you.

I look forward to seeing you tomorrow morning.

Kind regards

Maya Reynolds

Overbean Limited
Registered in England at 16 Wigland Place, Bradwell Road, Winscombe, WX12 6PP
Company No 4321101 42

Tel 0123 456789
Email maya@overbean.co.uk
www.overbean.co.uk

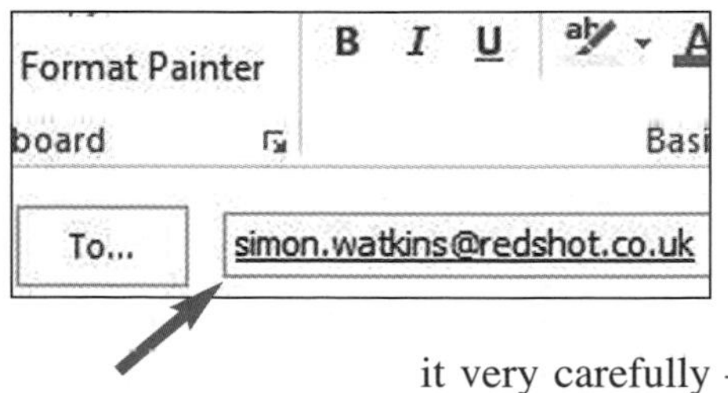

to whom are you sending it?

When you are addressing an email it is very important to get the person's email address correct. Email addresses can sometimes be quite complicated and may include names, numbers, dashes and full stops. Make sure when you are entering the recipient's email address that you do it very carefully – any mistake in keying it in and the email will not get to the right person, or may be returned as undeliverable.

replies

If you are replying to an email that you have received you can use the **reply function**. This is a quick way of replying to the sender and ensures that you are using the right email address and avoid typing errors.

The reply function should not be mixed up with the **reply all function**, as this will send your message to all the people who were copied in on the original email. This is fine if you want them all to see what you have written but should be used with caution – no one wants to be copied in on emails that are not relevant to them and you may end up sending the reply to people you do not want to receive it!

what is the subject?

The subject line is designed to draw the person's attention to what is included in the email. Look at the subject line below:

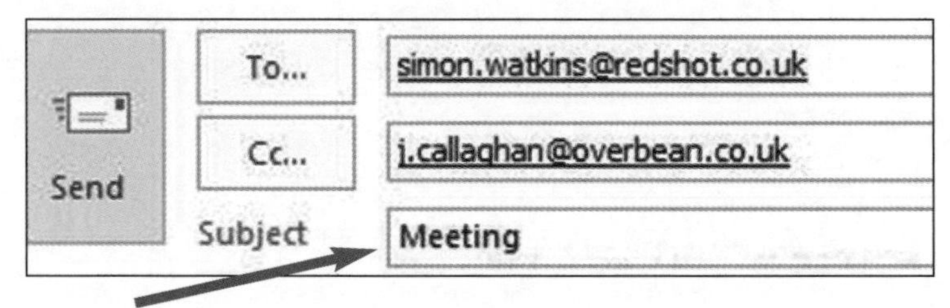

A vague subject line that says 'Meeting' does not give much of an idea of the details included. A better subject wording might be:

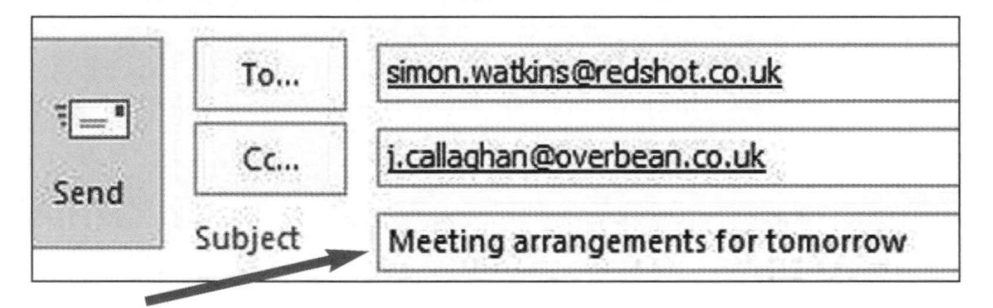

It is clear from this subject what the email is about: when the reader opens his/her inbox it will act as a reminder – ie do not forget the meeting! If the meeting had been further in the future a date might also be included.

copying in others

There is the option to copy other people in on an email that you send; this is the **Cc**, or **Carbon copy** line.

There will be certain situations where you want to send the same email to a number of people; perhaps they are all coming to the same meeting that you have organised. In this case you may decide to copy them all in to the same

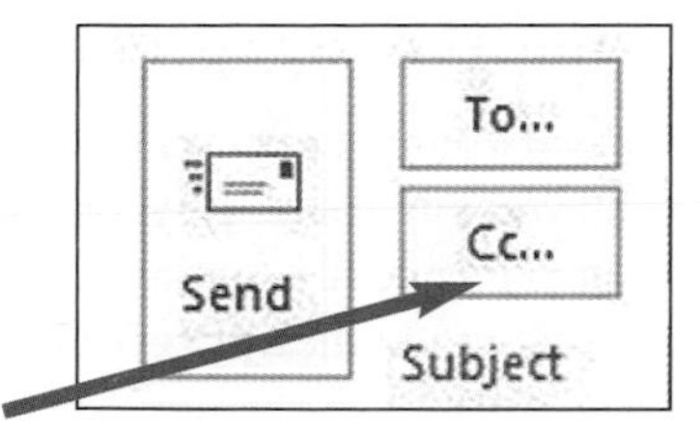

email and adding a number of email addresses to the Cc line is an efficient way of doing this.

If you decide to use the Cc function to copy others in to an email, remember that all the recipients will be able to see the other email addresses on the list. This is fine if they all work for the same organisation, but you must consider data protection and confidentiality if the other recipients do not know each other.

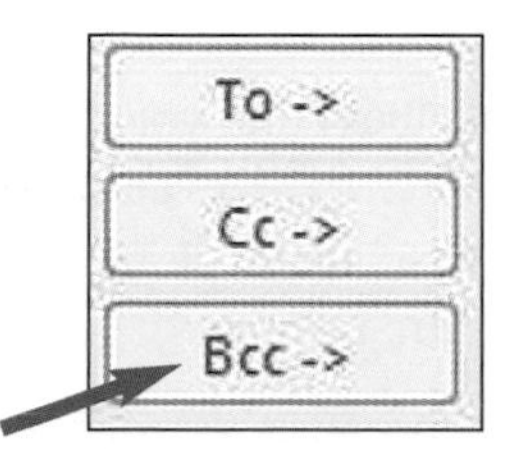

blind copying

In addition to Cc there is also the option to **Bcc** or **Blind carbon copy** an email. Like Cc this also allows you to copy the same email to a group of people, but in this case each member will not see the email addresses of other members of the group (this is why it is 'blind' copying).

WRITING THE EMAIL

using business language

In the last Chapter we saw that business communications are different from communications to friends, where texting has introduced a whole range of abbreviations and slang. Business communications on the other hand are:

- more formal
- more respectful
- more complex
- potentially clearer and more accurate

But business English is not a foreign language; it is no more difficult than the spoken English you use when talking to friends and family. It is just that you have to think more about the way you write or speak and remember with whom you are communicating; these people may be:

- working in the same business as you with a similar level of job
- working in the same business as you at a lower level
- a supervisor or manager
- working in a different business or organisation
- a customer

On the next couple of pages we will give examples of good practice in writing and sending emails.

addressing the person receiving the email

There are lots of ways in which you can start an email with what is known as a 'salutation'. With a friend you might say 'Hey' or 'Hi' because you know them well. When you are in a business situation it is important that you address the person you are writing to in the **appropriate** way. Here are some tips for what is appropriate:

- if it is someone you know well or who works at the same level or below you in the same organisation, then it is fine to use first names, ie 'Hello Scarlett', or 'Hi Scarlett'
- if it is someone external to the business that you do not know you should start with 'Dear Mr/Mrs/Miss/Ms ....' even if you are replying to an email that was signed with a first name, it is better to use a formal greeting to begin with, ie 'Dear Mrs Fallowes'
- there is often a temptation that because you are emailing rather than writing a formal letter it is acceptable to use more informal language or a more relaxed tone – if you are in any doubt about how to address someone in a business email, you should take a more formal approach

the content of the email

Once you have input the subject of the email there are a number of things that you need to remember when you actually write it:

- emails are designed to communicate information to the reader in an accurate and efficient way
- if you need to discuss an urgent matter with someone at work, it is better to speak to him or her in person
- equally, if you are trying to solve a problem or a complicated query that someone has, it is better to pick up the telephone and talk it through

when writing emails you should always...

✔ **keep it simple** – emails work best for providing straightforward answers to queries or for making simple requests; if an email ends up being very long then you probably should have communicated in a different way!

✔ **be clear about what you want** – if you are asking for information or for a response, make sure that this is made clear to the reader, for example 'please can I have the report by the end of the week' or 'please let me know when I can expect the information from you'

✔ **use bullet points** – if there are several points you are making, it is easier for the reader to deal with each point individually

✔ **use appropriate language** – it may seem obvious, but a business email should be written in appropriate business language, particularly if the email is being sent outside the business

✔ **proofread before sending** – make sure you check the spelling and grammar in your email before you send it

✔ **keep the email 'thread'** (ie all the emails that have gone before it) – if you are replying to an email you have received make sure the thread is still included with the email otherwise the content of your email may not make sense

✔ **be polite** – if someone sends you an email, thank them for it; if you consider you owe an apology for something, for example a late or forgotten reply, a slip up in communication or a mistake, apologise for it – also note that critical or personal remarks and comments are not appropriate in a business email (or in any business dealings)

some email warnings...

✗ **NEVER USE WORDS ALL IN CAPITAL LETTERS** within the text – putting text in capitals is known as 'shouting' and completely out of place in written communications

✗ do not use a lot of **exclamation marks!!!!!!** – while it's fine to use these in personal emails to indicate surprise or humour, these should be avoided in formal work emails

✗ do not use **emoticons** - these should only be used in personal communications

✗ do not try and make **jokes** – something that sounds funny when you say it to someone may not come across as funny when it is written down; in fact it could be taken the wrong way and offend somebody

- ✗ avoid **slang** – this can sound casual and disrespectful
- ✗ avoid **language that might upset** – swear words and comments that are not politically correct can be very upsetting to people who are sensitive about these issues

signing off the email (complimentary close)

There are different ways of signing off an email (a 'complimentary close'), but business etiquette requires that you should provide an email sign off that:

- is appropriate
- shows respect for the person getting the email
- reflects the salutation (ie the 'Dear Mr Cameron') at the start of the email

The examples below show some possible ways of starting and finishing off emails in different situations.

Important note! These examples are only an approximate guide because businesses vary greatly – some are formal in the way employees deal with each other and address each other and some are informal. The examples shown here are more formal, so do not worry if the terms you use are different. If you are in any doubt, use the more formal terms.

suggested email salutations and sign offs – internal emails

situation	salutation	sign off
a work colleague you know	*Hi/Hello + first name*	*Thanks, Cheers*
a colleague at your level you don't know	*Hello/Dear + first name*	*Regards, Thanks*
a supervisor/manager at work you talk to using their first name	*Hi/Hello + first name*	*Regards*

suggested email salutations and sign offs – external emails

emailing another business	salutation	sign off
a person at your level you know	*Hi/Hello + first name*	*Regards*
a person at your level you don't know	*Dear + first name*	*Kind regards, Regards*
a manager whose name you know	*Dear Mr/Mrs/Miss/Ms + family name*	*Kind regards, Yours sincerely*
emailing a customer	**salutation**	**sign off**
a customer whose name you know	*Dear Mr/Mrs/Miss/Ms + family name*	*Yours sincerely, Kind regards*
a customer whose name you don't know	*Dear Sir/Madam*	*Yours faithfully Kind regards, Regards*

sending attachments

Emails are also an efficient way of sending documents electronically. In the workplace these documents might include an agenda for a meeting, a list of suppliers, or a spreadsheet that analyses monthly sales information.

Any electronic document can be attached to an email and sent to the recipient. If the document is in paper format it can be scanned and sent. In the case of the sample email shown on the second page of this chapter, Maya Reynolds is sending Simon Watkins an agenda for a meeting and a map of how to get to the meeting.

Lastly, two golden rules for sending attachments:

- make sure the file size for the attachment(s) is not too large
- **most importantly – do not forget to attach the attachment!**

adding security to attached documents

When sending emails there is always a risk that if the attachment contains sensitive or confidential information it might fall into the wrong hands. In order to keep confidential information safe it is a good idea to **password protect** the document before it is sent. In other words, you will need to create a password for the recipient to be able to open the document. This password should be sent to the recipient separately. The screen below illustrates password protection of a pdf file. Similar routines can be found in the 'Help' functions in other software, including Microsoft Word.

Encryption Level: 128-bit AES

Select Document Components to Encrypt

- (●) Encrypt all document contents
- ( ) Encrypt all document contents except metadata (Acrobat 6 and later compatible)
- ( ) Encrypt only file attachments (Acrobat 7 and later compatible)

All contents of the document will be encrypted and search engines will not be able to access the document's metadata.

☑ Require a password to open the document

Document Open Password: •••••••

This password will be required to open the document.

Permissions

☑ Restrict editing and printing of the document. A password will be required in order to change these permission settings.

Change Permissions Password: •••••••

Printing Allowed: None

Changes Allowed: None

IMPROVING EMAILS

One of the things you may be asked to do in your assessment for this Unit is to review an email and decide how it could be improved. We will now look at a Case Study below to see how this might be done.

Case Study

THE HIGHBRIDGE GROUP – IMPROVING EMAILS

situation

Ollie Castle works as an assistant in the Customer Services Team at the Head Office of The Highbridge Group. The business runs three luxury hotels in the area. He is relatively new to the job and is still being trained in the role.

Ollie has received an email from a potential customer, Samera Malik from Rowfields Ltd. Ollie has drafted a reply but has asked you to check it for him before he sends it. Read the emails below and decide what improvements could be made to Ollie's reply.

message from Samera Malik, Sales Manager:

To:	customerservices@thehighbridgegroup.com
From:	s.malik@rowfields.com
Date:	Tuesday, 10 April 20XX, 09.28
Subject:	Conference booking for Rowfields Ltd

Dear Sir/Madam,

I am considering using your Hathaway Hotel in Stratford for a corporate conference I am organising in the Spring next year. All delegates will need rooms for a two-night stay. I will also need use of your main conference room and several smaller meeting rooms. I have looked at the pricing on your website and think that it is too high for what you are offering.

Please can you arrange for someone to call me to discuss this in more detail and with details of what improvement you can offer on the prices on your website.

Thank you for your help with this.

Regards

Ms Samera Malik
Sales Manager, Rowfields Ltd
s.malik@rowfields.com
01234 987654

draft reply from Ollie Castle:

To:	s.malik@rofields.com
From:	customerservices@thehighbridgegroup.com
Date:	Tuesday, 10 April 20XX, 10.30
Subject:	Re: Conference booking for Rowfields Ltd

Hi Samera,

Thanks for your email about using our Stratford hotel for your conference. I know our prices seem a bit steep but you get what you pay for and maybe you don't normally use somewhere as posh as us!!!

I'm sure we can sought something out about the price, but b4 I pass your query on to one of the sales team purhaps you can give me an idea of how much you want to spend on the conference and I'll see what I can do :-)

We look forward to hearing from you soon.

Cheers

Ollie

solution

These are the issues that should be raised with Ollie Castle:

- Ollie has used 'Hi' as his greeting in the email – this is too familiar, as he has not met Samera Malik and she has addressed him formally as 'Dear Sir'. He should have started the email 'Dear Ms Malik' as she is a manager at Rowfields Ltd and needs to be given some respect.
- Ollie has used 'Cheers' as his sign off in the email – this is also too familiar. He should use something formal like 'Regards' or 'Kind regards'.
- Ollie should not comment 'you get what you pay for' and certainly should not comment on whether Ms Malik does or does not normally use 'posh' hotels, as this is rude. Instead he should pass her email on to someone in the sales team who can discuss her requirements with her.
- There is no need for the '!!!' at the end of the first paragraph – exclamation marks should be used very sparingly, if at all.
- The abbreviation b4 is 'text speak' and should be written 'before'.
- **:-)** is too familiar – emoticons should not be used in business emails.
- There are three spelling mistakes:
  - – Ms Malik's email address has a 'w' missing – the email would never reach her
  - – 'sought' should be 'sort'
  - – 'purhaps' should be 'perhaps'

Chapter Summary

- Emails are increasingly being used by businesses to communicate both internally with other employees and externally with other businesses and customers.

- Great care needs to be taken with email addresses: if you get one wrong it may go to the wrong person or it may be returned as undeliverable.

- As emails are short they need to be very clear and accurate and state the subject of the message on the subject line very concisely.

- Care must also be taken when copying in groups of people to emails, as email addresses can be confidential information. The option of Blind copying (Bc) will ensure that individual members of a group that is emailed will not see the addresses of the other members.

- Business language must be used when sending business emails. This means that the language used is more formal and shows respect to the recipient. It does not mean that the language is more difficult or complicated. It should still be easy to understand.

- The features of a good business email are that:
  - it should be simple
  - it should be polite and respectful
  - you state clearly what you have to say in appropriate language
  - it can include bullet points
  - it should be checked before sending

- A business email should not:
  - use text in CAPITAL LETTERS
  - use exclamation marks!!!!!!!!!
  - use emoticons such as smileys
  - contain jokes and attempted humour
  - contain upsetting language, eg swearing or politically incorrect comments

- Care must be taken in writing business emails when using salutations (eg 'Dear Mr . . .') and complimentary closes (eg 'Kind regards', 'Best wishes') so that they are appropriate to the recipient.

- Business emails can often be sent with attached files, eg Word files and pictures. Great care must be taken to ensure that the files are not too large, and also that they are actually attached.

- If a business email has an attachment which contains sensitive or confidential information it may be security protected with a password for opening it.

Key Terms

reply function	the email function which enables you to send a reply to the recipient without having to key in the email address
reply all function	the email function which enables you to send the reply to everyone copied in on the original email
subject line	the field in an email where you enter a clear description of the email that you are sending
Carbon copy (Cc)	the option for you to copy an email you are sending to one or more other people
Blind copy (Bc)	the option for you to copy an email you are sending to one or more other people so that each person copied in does not see the email addresses of the other people being copied in
business language	language used for business communications – it is more formal and respectful than the ordinary spoken English or the abbreviated English used in texting and in personal emails
salutation	the greeting which goes before the main text of an email, eg 'Dear Mr . . .'
complimentary close	the wording used to sign off an email, eg 'Kind regards'
email thread	if you are doing a reply, all the emails that have come before that reply
emoticons	a symbol of your feelings in the form of a human face (eg smiley face, sad face) embodied in the text
attachment	an electronic file sent with an email
document security	the process of setting up security settings – such as password protection – within an electronic file in order to protect sensitive or confidential material

2.1 Business emails should only be used to communicate with other people in the same organisation.

	✔
(a) True	
(b) False	

2.2 Decide which of the following options for the subject line of an email is the most appropriate.

	✔
(a) Subject: Agenda	
(b) Subject: Agenda for the meeting on Monday 12 March at 2.30pm for all the sales team and the customer services team	
(c) Subject: Team meeting Agenda 2.30pm 12/03/20XX	
(d) Subject: Team meeting agenda	

2.3 Complete the following sentences by selecting one of the options shown in bold type below (use each option once).

blind **carbon** **all**

none **carbon**

'If you use the .... copy function, ... of the recipients of the email will be able to see the other email addresses on the list.'

'If you use the .... copy function, ... of the recipients of the email will be able to see the other email addresses on the list.'

2.4 For each of the following decide whether it is something that you should do, or should avoid, when writing a business email.

	should do ✔	**should avoid** ✔
Keep the email simple		
Use capital letters to emphasise a point		
Use exclamation marks to indicate surprise		
Be clear about what you want		
Use bullet points		
Check the grammar and spelling		
Use emoticons		
Keep the email thread going		
Make jokes or use humour		
Use slang words		

2.5 Decide in which of the following circumstances it is appropriate to use an email for business communication. Tick all that apply.

		✔
(a)	To explain to a friend why you will be unable to meet up for a drink that evening	
(b)	To send confidential information which is in a password-protected document	
(c)	To arrange with your five colleagues who is going to get the next round of coffees in your office	
(d)	To send the arrangements for the next office team meeting to the ten members of the team	
(e)	To reply to a customer email asking for the address and telephone number of your business's Customer Services Department	
(f)	To place an order for more paper for the office photocopier	

2.6 Carina Garcia works as an administrative assistant at Fastprint Ltd, a business that produces printed clothing for music festivals, concerts and sports events. She has received the following email from a music festival organiser and has drafted a reply. Before sending it she has asked you to take a look at it and provide her with feedback. You should:

(a) identify and list errors that she has made, eg spelling errors and poor business etiquette

(b) write an appropriate revised email reply to Fraser which corrects these errors

Message from Fraser Bales, Festival Director:

To: admin@fastprint.com
From: fraserbales@gosford-festivals.com
Date: Monday, 25 July 20XX, 10.15

Subject: Festival T-shirts

Dear Carina,

Order number: 42478/gosfes

We have received the T-shirts we ordered from you for the music festival that starts on Friday 29 July. The colour of the t-shirts is definitely not the shade of blue that we specified in our order; it is much lighter. I am really concerned about this so can you please arrange for someone senior in your organisation to call me as soon as possible to discuss this issue.

Thank you for your help with this.

Fraser Bales
Festival Director, Gosford Festivals
fraserbales@gosford-festivals.com
07070 135790

Draft reply from Carina Garcia:

To: fraserbales@gosford-festivals.com
Cc: m.worthington@fastprint.com
From: admin@fastprint.com
Date: Monday, 25 July 20XX, 10.30

Subject: Re: Festival T-shirts

Hi Fraser,

Order number: 24478/gosfes

Oh dear!! That's not good!!! Is it a nice shade of blue? If it is I'm sure no one will notise. Marcus, the Operations Manager, is off today but will be back in the office tomorrow. I've copied him in on this email so I'm sure he'll give you a buzz sometime when he's free.

The weather looks dry for the weekend so it should be a good festivel. Have a good one!

Carina

www.fastprint.com
01399 235212

2.7 Read the email below together with the note that follows and then draft a suitable email reply for Elijah Banks to send to the customer. Use the format shown at the bottom of the page.

Message from Maurice Jeffries, a customer

To: elijahbanks@fabulous-footwear.com
From: mauricejeffries@warmmail.com
Date: Tuesday, 07 February 20XX, 11.28

Subject: Men's shoes, Customer reference 47346MJ

Dear Elijah Banks,

Thank you for the new catalogue you sent me in the post today, I got your name from the covering letter. There is a pair of brown men's shoes that I particularly like on page 24; they are the item marked (h). Please can you help me with the sizing as they are marked in European sizing but I am only familiar with UK sizes.

Thank you for your help with this.

Regards

Maurice Jeffries

01297 413784

Note: there is a chart that converts European sizes to UK sizes at the back of the Fabulous Footwear catalogue on page 48.

To:
From:
Date:
Subject:

3 Business letters

this chapter covers...

This chapter explains how to write a simple and professional business letter. The topics covered are:

- *the difference between emails and letters*
- *the structure of a standard business letter*
- *the individual parts of a business letter and how they can differ depending on what the letter is about and who will be receiving it*
- *the style of a business letter*
- *practical examples and hints on 'how to write a business letter' concentrating on the main message ('body') of the letter*
- *getting the language right*
- *using standard letters*

EMAILS AND LETTERS

the increasing use of emails

We saw in the last chapter that emails have now become one of the main ways in which people and businesses communicate with each other. Before emails were introduced in the early 1980s the letter was the main form of written communication. But, as we will see in this chapter, letters are still used by businesses in some situations.

letters

Businesses use letters in a limited number of situations to communicate with the **public**. Examples include:

- job offers from employers
- letters from utility companies to persuade you to switch provider
- covering letters to supplement advertising material

Letters are also used as a form of communication between **businesses** and other **businesses**. Examples include:

- advertising of goods and services
- contracts, terms and conditions for the supply of goods or services
- letters chasing overdue accounts

emails or letters?

You will see from the examples above that letters are **more formal** and official than emails and will generally **make more impression**.

Also a printed piece of paper is more 'real' than an email which appears on a computer screen for possibly a few seconds, or may not even make it onto the screen if it has been deleted as 'spam' or is of no interest at all to the person receiving it.

The **main differences** between a letter and an email are therefore:

- a letter is normally a more formal document than an email
- the language used in a letter is generally more formal than the language used in an email
- a letter takes longer to prepare than an email and longer to reach its destination
- a letter is less commonly used than an email in a business office
- a letter can often have more impact than an email

THE STRUCTURE OF A BUSINESS LETTER

An example of a typical business letter is shown on the next page. Study the various parts of the letter and read the notes set out below.

example – business letter

This letter has been sent by Mr A L Binoni, Accounts Manager of Deliziosi Chocolates to the Grand Royal Hotel in Exmouth. He is chasing up an overdue invoice and demanding that a payment of £499.50 should be made to his business bank account.

printed letterhead	The name and address of the business is normally already printed on the letter.
the date	The date is entered in date (number), month (word), year (number) order.
reference	This is used for filing purposes by the company sending the letter.
name and address of the recipient	The name and address of the person to whom the letter is sent.
salutation (greeting)	'Dear Sir. . . Dear Madam' – if you know the person's name and title (ie Mr, Mrs, Miss, Ms) use it, but check that it is correct.
subject of letter	This is what the letter is all about.
body of letter	The body of the letter is where the message of the letter is set out. The text must: – be laid out in short precise paragraphs and short clear sentences – start with a point of reference (eg referring to the invoice) – set out the message in a logical sequence – be written in plain English with no slang or complicated words
complimentary close (sign off)	The complimentary close (signing off phrase) must be consistent with the salutation: 'Dear Sir' is followed by 'Yours faithfully'. If a name was included in the salutation, the sign off would be 'Yours sincerely'.
signature of sender	This space is normally left blank for an authorised person's signature.
name of sender	The name will be followed by the job title of the sender.
'enc'	This is short for 'enclosures' and means that documents are enclosed (in this case the statement of account and a copy of the unpaid invoice)

Deliziosi Chocolates
79 West Street
London
WC2H 9NQ
Tel 020 77836 1066
email sales@deliziosichocs.co.uk

15 December 20XX

Ref AB/567

The General Manager
Grand Royal Hotel
17 Sandys Road
Exmouth
EX8 7DT

Dear Sir

Invoice 19831 £499.50

We note from our records that we have not yet received payment of our invoice 19831 dated 15 September 20XX. Our latest statement of account is enclosed, together with a copy of the invoice.

Our payment terms are strictly 30 days from the date of the invoice. We shall be grateful if you will settle the £499.50 without further delay.

We look forward to receiving your BACS payment (account: Deliziosi Chocolates, Capital Bank, Strand Branch, Account number 82744163, sort code 83-99-15).

Yours faithfully

A L Binoni

A L Binoni
Accounts Manager
enc

the 'house style' business letter

If you have seen business letters – maybe in a work experience placement or if you have received one – you will know that businesses set out each letter in the same uniform 'house' style. This gives the letter a particular 'look' which identifies the business and is common to all the letters that it sends. This 'look' can involve the use of standard printed stationery showing the logo, name, address and details of the business, and it will be set out with headings, paragraphs, signatures in a uniform way.

features of a fully blocked letter

There are a number of different ways of setting out the main text of a letter. The most common of these – the 'fully blocked' style – is the style illustrated on the previous page. The features of this 'fully blocked' style are:

- it is the most commonly used style of letter
- all the lines start at the left margin
- it uses open punctuation, ie there is no punctuation except in the main body of the letter, which uses normal punctuation
- paragraphs are divided by a double space, and are not indented
- a fully blocked letter is easy to type as all the lines are set uniformly to the left margin

WRITING THE LETTER

the relatively easy bits

You will see on the previous page that there are a lot of details that have to go on the letter. These can be fiddly but are reasonably straightforward:

- the **date** . . . 15 December 20XX . . . this is easy to deal with
- the **reference** . . . Ref AB/567 . . . the initials of the writer followed by a number used for filing away the letter
- the **name and address of the recipient** . . . this is also easy
- the **salutation (greeting)** . . . Dear Sir . . . this can be more tricky: if you don't know the person's name, write 'Dear Sir' (or 'Dear Madam' if it is a female); if you do know the name, use it but make sure you get it right!
- the **subject** . . . Invoice 19831 £499.50 . . . this is must be short and concise, as here, and it must be accurate

- the **complimentary close** . . . Yours faithfully . . . this is must be short and to the point, as here, and it must be accurate. Remember:
  - if you start the letter with 'Dear Sir' or 'Dear Madam' (ie with no name) it must end with 'Yours faithfully'
  - if you start the letter with a name eg 'Dear Mrs Cameron' it must end with 'Yours sincerely'
- **signature, name, enc** . . . these are easy to deal with

the difficult bit – knowing what to write

The part of the letter which can prove difficult is writing the text in the body of the letter. It can help if you think of the letter being in numbered stages.

The example letter below uses a business situation which you can follow through by reading the text in italics. The letter is a complaint about a faulty printer.

DELTA ENTERPRISES
3 Helicon Way
Paradise Road
Birmingham B4 8GG

20 December 20XX

Dear Sir

1 details of previous contact (if there has been contact):

'Further to my order for a printer (Ref P8742) placed on 1 July,'

2 your reason for writing:

'I am writing to complain about the quality of the equipment I received from you.'

3 the main point of the letter:

'The printer I ordered was defective: it did not pick up the paper properly from the paper tray and kept jamming. Also the photographs I printed out were very poor quality.'

4 asking for action to be taken (if it is needed):

'Please send a replacement printer as soon as possible.'

5 closing remarks:

'I look forward to receiving this item'

Yours faithfully

Charlie Sampson

Manager

Your AAT assessment may ask you to draft the text of a short letter dealing with an enquiry or a problem which is reported to you.

The Case Study below shows an example of a problem and a letter that is written to put the situation right.

Case Study

ZODIAC SUPPLIES – A DISCOUNT ERROR

Azhar Saleem works in the Accounts Department of Henson Systems, a website design company. He is checking invoices sent to his company by Zodiac Supplies which provides Henson Systems with computer equipment. He notices that Invoice 6743, dated 30 October 20XX, shows goods costing £500 with a trade discount of only £50 (ie 10%) rather than the £75 (15%) which has been agreed.

On 1 December 20XX Azhar emails Zodiac Supplies pointing out the error and asks for a formal letter to be sent to Henson Systems confirming the 15% discount. The letter should be addressed to Harbir Singh, Accounts Supervisor, Henson Systems, Unit 1D, Evergreen Estate, Melchester ME4 7GH.

You work for Zodiac Supplies and have been asked to write the requested letter, for signature by Jim Barrie, Accounts Supervisor. The text of your letter is shown below.

Harbir Singh, Accounts Supervisor
Henson Systems, Unit 1D, Evergreen Estate
Melchester, ME4 7GH

3 December 20XX
Ref JB/846

Dear Mr Singh

Invoice 6743

I am writing in response to Azhar Saleem's email of 1 December pointing out that we have given the wrong discount on Invoice 6743.

Please accept our apologies for this error.

I confirm that our agreed terms are for a trade discount of 15% rather than 10%, and payment within 30 days of the invoice.

I attach a credit note for the overcharge on invoice 6743.

Yours sincerely

Jim Barrie
Accounts Supervisor
enc

the stages of writing the letter – a recap

If you read the letter in the Case Study you can see that it is written in the series of 'stages' explained on page 39.

These are summarised as follows:

Dear Mr Singh

1 details of previous contact

'I am writing in response to Azhar Saleem's email of 1 December pointing out that we have given the wrong discount on Invoice 6743.'

2 your reason for writing:

Please accept our apologies for this error.

3 the main point of the letter:

I confirm that our agreed terms are for a trade discount of 15% rather than 10%, and payment within 30 days of the invoice.

4 asking for action to be taken:

(none in this case - it is an apology)

5 closing remarks:

I attach a credit note for the overcharge on invoice 6743.

Yours sincerely

Jim Barrie

GETTING THE LANGUAGE RIGHT

what is 'formal' language?

As explained in the beginning of this chapter, the language used when writing business letters should be **formal**.

But 'formal' can be a misleading word as people associate it with dressing up for special occasions such as weddings and proms. Language should not be 'dressed up' by using long 'posh sounding' words.

'Formal' language simply means that the language used should:

- give a clear message
- use simple words

- use short sentences
- use a new paragraph at the start of each new subject (as in the 'stages' of the letter shown on page 40)
- avoid slang and 'text speak' abbreviations

The Case Study which now follows gives two examples of the use of language:

- **informal language** (the **wrong** way to write a business letter)
- **formal language** (the **correct** way to write a business letter)

Case Study

HENSON SYSTEMS LTD – A JOB APPLICATION

You are Edward Henson, Director of Henson Systems Ltd, a major website design company. On 14 February you receive a letter from Olivia Powell, a Computer Science student at the local college. She is looking for employment and is interested in working for your business as she is impressed with your website. The text of her letter is as follows:

10 February 20XX

Dear Mr Henson

Employment opportunities

I am currently looking for employment in the area of computer programming. I am just completing a diploma in Computer Science at Holywell College and have seen your website and also the websites of your clients and find them very interesting and impressive.

Please could you send me details of how to apply for a job with your company. I attach a CV for your information.

I look forward to hearing from you.

Yours sincerely

O M Powell

Olivia Powell (Miss)

enc

You ask Bev Winsome, a temp assisting you while your secretary is on maternity leave, to draft a letter for your signature. Bev says 'Oh yes, I know Liv all right. We were at school together.'

The company's normal procedure is to send out a formal letter with an application form to job applicants, who are also asked to send a CV.

Later in the day, Bev gives you her draft which reads as follows:

> Dear Liv
>
> Thanks for your letter.
>
> Here is an application form for you to fill in. It might be a good idea 4 you to send along a CV as well, although it's not always neccesary.
>
> Best
>
> *Bev Winsome*
>
> B Winsome, Assistant to Mr Hensome

You are not very happy with this draft. You tell Bev that you expect letters to be written in appropriate business language and not contain so many mistakes.

The problems with Bev's draft are:

1 The letter should be addressed to 'Miss Powell' and not 'Liv'.

2 The 'Thanks for your letter' is too casual and lacks detail.

3 The letter contains 'text speak' such as '4' instead of 'for'.

4 'Neccesary' is incorrectly spelt; it should be 'necessary'.

5 Bev has missed the fact that a CV has already been sent.

6 The letter is signed off 'Best' when it should have been 'Yours sincerely'.

7 The letter should be for your signature and not signed by Bev.

8 The letter has quoted your name ('Henson') as 'Hensome'.

You decide to dictate a new letter written in correct business English with all of Bev's errors corrected. The text is as follows:

> Dear Miss Powell
>
> Thank you for your letter of 10 February 20XX and your interest in an employment position with our company.
>
> I am pleased to enclose an application form and will be grateful if you would complete it and send it back to me. You do not need to send a further CV.
>
> I look forward to hearing from you.
>
> Yours sincerely
>
> *Edward Henson*
>
> Edward Henson
>
> Director

The result was a success: Olivia Powell got a job with Henson Systems.

STANDARD LETTERS

Businesses often use **standard letters** – using the same wording – for situations which are repeated over and over again. You will encounter these if you are working in an accounting and business environment. They include external and internal letters:

external letters

- to accompany catalogues sent to customers
- sent to customers to announce new products
- notifying customers when a credit account is opened in their name, giving details of credit limit, payment terms etc
- chasing credit customers who do not pay their invoices
- advising customers of public holiday opening times

internal letters

- to accompany renewal contracts of employment
- to announce pay rises
- to announce possible redundancies
- termination of employment contract letters

advantages of standard letters

There are a number of advantages of using standard letters:

- because the wording is the same each time you can be fairly sure that it is **correct for the situation** – and so no errors or misunderstandings will occur
- because the wording is set in advance you do not have to write the main text of the letter yourself – this saves time and effort
- if temps or new staff are employed they will be able to send out these letters without having to learn how to write them – this saves time and money that otherwise would have to be spent on training

standard letters and emails

You should note that the same principles apply to emails as well as to letters. As businesses use emails more frequently and letters less often, the use of **standard emails** both internally and externally will greatly improve the efficiency of the organisation.

Chapter Summary

- Emails are increasingly being used by businesses to communicate both internally and externally.
- Letters are becoming far less common but are still used both internally and externally.
- Business letters are generally more formal than emails and will often make more impact as they are more permanent.
- The language used in letters is generally more formal than the language used in emails.
- A business letter often has a pre-printed 'header' with the name, logo and contact details of the business.
- The rest of the business letter has a defined structure including:
  - date
  - reference
  - name and address of recipient
  - greeting (Dear . . . .etc), also known as the 'salutation'
  - subject of letter
  - body of the letter (the main text)
  - sign off (Yours sincerely . . . etc), also known as the 'complimentary close'
  - the signature and name of the sender
  - 'enc' (ie enclosures)
- Business letters are generally in a defined 'house style' which gives the business an identity which is easily recognised by the reader.
- The body of a business letter is the most difficult part to write because it involves a formal structure and a number of stages in the following order:
  - details of any earlier contact
  - telling the reader what the letter is about and why you are writing
  - setting out the main point(s) and details
  - asking for action to be taken (if required)
  - closing off the letter in a polite way
- The text of a business letter needs to be clear and detailed. This will be helped by using simple words, short sentences and new paragraphs for new subjects.
- Businesses often use standard 'fixed wording' letters for situations which occur regularly.

Key Terms

business letter	a letter written specifically for sending internally within a business or externally to other businesses or customers
formal language	the language used in a business letter – it must be clear, not using obscure or very long words, and also avoiding slang or 'text' words
recipient	the person or business receiving the letter
salutation	the greeting to the recipient – eg 'Dear Mr . . .', which must be appropriate to that recipient
complimentary close	the 'sign off' phrase at the end of the letter before the name and signature of the sender – eg 'Yours sincerely . . .' – it must be appropriate to the salutation: – 'Dear Sir' (ie no name given) is followed by 'Yours faithfully' – 'Dear Mr Box' (a name is given) is followed by 'Yours sincerely'
enc	this is short for 'enclosed' and means that the letter is sent with one or more documents
house style	this means that the 'style' of the letter sent is always the same and gives the business sending it a recognisable identity which the reader will know or get to know – 'style' can include features such as a logo shown on a printed letterhead and the way the letter is set out, and its use of colour
fully blocked letter	this is a common format for a business letter – features include all the text starting on the left margin (ie no indentation), spaces between paragraphs, and punctuation only in the body of the letter

3.1 Consider the following statements which compare letters and emails. Decide whether they are true or false and tick the appropriate column in the table.

	True ✔	False ✔
An email is more formal than a business letter		
The language used in a letter is generally more formal than an email		
A letter can often have more impact than an email		
A letter takes less time to prepare than an email		
A letter is less commonly used than an email in a business office		

3.2 The lay-out of a business letter that identifies the business and is used for all letters that the business sends is known as which of the following? Select one option.

		✔
(a)	Standard format	
(b)	House style	
(c)	Covering letter	
(d)	Formal letter	

3.3 Complete the following sentences by selecting the correct word from the two options shown below.

sincerely **faithfully**

A letter that starts 'Dear Sir' or 'Dear Madam' should end with the complimentary close 'Yours ....'

A letter that starts 'Dear Mrs Llewellyn' should end with the complimentary close 'Yours ....'

3.4 Write down in the numbered table below the following elements of a business letter in the order in which they normally appear:

- Date
- Subject of the letter
- Complimentary close
- Printed letterhead
- Name of the sender
- Body of the letter
- Signature of the sender
- Reference
- Salutation
- Enclosures
- Name and address of the recipient

1	
2	
3	
4	
5	
6	
7	
8	
9	
10	
11	

3.5 You are Jamie Outhwaite, a Customer Services Assistant at Harold & Howe, a building supplier in Graysville. You have received the following letter:

27 Foxwell Avenue
Graysville
GY22 2PP

4 June, 20XX

Dear Harold & Howe,

I am currently planning an extension to my house, which I will be building myself. I need a copy of your current catalogue and price list so that I can calculate the cost of the supplies that I will need. I cannot find anywhere on your website where I can request a catalogue or a price list and the ones that I have are out of date. Please send me this information as soon as possible.

Yours sincerely,

J Wenderbury

Mr Jonathan Wenderbury
Customer reference JW19327

You have worked for Harold & Howe for eighteen months and in that time there has never been a printed catalogue or a price list for customers. It is suggested to anyone who requests a catalogue or price list that they visit the website www.h&hsupplies.com and download the documents.

You are to write a letter in response to Mr Wenderbury's letter. The organisation's letterhead (ie the business name, address and contact details) is shown below. Your answer (not including the letterhead) should be approximately 90 to 140 words. It is suggested that you use the elements shown in the house style set out on page 37 of this chapter.

Harold & Howe
Unit 5, Drayton Industrial Estate
Maynard Road
Graysville
GY14 4LG
telephone: 04164 445566
email: custserv@h&hsupplies.com

3.6 Harold & Howe have recently employed a temporary member of staff, Roland Berger, to cover the reception desk and to help with some of the customer services work.

Roland is excellent in the reception role, but his written communication is less good. Harold & Howe have received a letter from Miss Jenna Patel and Roland has drafted a reply. He has shown you both letters and asked for your feedback before sending the letter.

Read the communications that took place between Roland and Miss Jenna Patel and then answer the questions that follow.

19A Green Lane, Graysville, GY3 1NP
Mob 09976542866

14 June, 20XX

Dear Sir or Madam,

Invoice 47263 - conservatory folding doors £2,560

I have recently received a reminder from your company regarding the above invoice with the threat of legal action if I fail to pay. The invoice is for the conservatory folding doors that I ordered in March that were delivered on 9 May. I spoke to a member of your staff last week and I explained that the doors were faulty; when I installed them they would not close properly. He assured me that he would arrange for someone from Harold & Howe to come and investigate the issue and that I should not have to pay the invoice until the issue has been resolved.

Please can you investigate this matter to make sure that Harold & Howe do not take legal action.

I look forward to hearing from you soon.

Yours faithfully

J Patel

Miss Jenna Patel

Customer reference JP19319A

Harold & Howe
Unit 5, Drayton Industrial Estate
Maynard Road
Graysville
GY14 4LG
telephone: 04164 445566
email: custserv@h&hsupplies.com

17 June 20XX

Dear Jenna,

Invoice 47263 - conservatory folding doors £2,560

Thanks for your leter. I have had a chat with our Credit Control department who say that you have about three weeks to pay before they take legal action. Are you sure that you are up to fiting these doors yourself as they are very heavy for a lady to do on her own. Maybe they are not correctly positioned. I would recomend that you get a professional builder to help.

If you can remember the name of the person here that you spoke to maybe you can call him directly and discuss it.

Yours faithfully

Indicate in the table below with a tick whether the statements relating to Roland's letter are true or false.

		True ✔	False ✔
(a)	The level of familiarity of the salutation (greeting) Roland uses is inappropriate		
(b)	There is more than one spelling mistake in Roland's letter		
(c)	It is appropriate for Roland to comment on Jenna Patel's ability to fit the conservatory doors herself as she is having problems		
(d)	Roland should have offered to find out who Jenna Patel spoke to himself and investigate the situation further		
(e)	The complimentary close (sign off) is appropriate and matches the salutation		
(f)	It is acceptable to use the emoticon as Roland is signing off with his first name only		
(g)	Roland should have included his full name and job title below his signature		

4 Telephones in business

this chapter covers...

This chapter describes the important role played by the telephone in business communications and the need to use the telephone in an appropriate way. The topics covered are:

- *the importance of telephone communications in business*
- *the increasing use of mobile phones*
- *telephones used within a business or externally when communicating with other businesses and customers*
- *the importance of knowing when a telephone call is appropriate to the circumstances and when it is not appropriate*
- *the need to communicate on the telephone in a professional and polite manner – following business etiquette*
- *the need to follow the policies and procedures of the business when speaking on the phone*
- *the use and misuse of 'scripted' telephone calls*

TELEPHONES IN BUSINESS

the use of phones in business – an overview

The growth in the use of phones inevitably affects the ways that businesses communicate with other businesses and also with customers.

We will firstly take an overview of the ways in which phones are used in business and then later in the chapter examine the 'phone etiquette' which should be observed by people working in business:

- a **fixed landline system** based on a wired connection to a switchboard and a number of extensions is central to many businesses
- **mobile phones** based on radio signals are now extremely common both within the office and also outside it and provide maximum flexibility to a business which relies on communication with employees working from home or on the move
- **mobile twinning** is the best of both worlds as you are contactable both on a landline and also on your mobile using the same number

The following advertising material for mobile twinning explains this well:

Mobile twinning

Why sit at your desk all day waiting to take calls? You do not need to!

If you spend time attending meetings and events, or are travelling between client consultations you should adopt mobile twinning.

Mobile twinning allows you to treat your mobile as if it were an extension of your desk phone, always being contactable on the same extension number, maintaining high levels of customer services and doing away with the telephone 'ping pong' that starts up when you try to get in contact with someone who is never there when you ring.

the increasing need for mobile phones

In an age in which people run their lives at an increasingly hectic pace there is a tendency to rely more and more on mobile phones to communicate. People increasingly expect an immediate response to text messages, voicemails, emails, Facebook posts and tweets. Tomorrow will not do if an answer is required and can be given today.

All these forms of communication can be carried out on today's smartphone, which has become a powerful and flexible tool for getting things done. But the mobile phone has also placed greater strains on the need to maintain business etiquette, as we will see later in this chapter.

internal and external use of the telephone

As with other forms of communication, the telephone – whether landline or mobile – can be used for **internal** and **external** contact:

- with people working for the same business – this is **internal contact** – the person being contacted can be inside the office or working somewhere else, for example at a meeting, a training course, while travelling or at home; this is where the mobile phone has greatly increased the efficiency of communication within a business as employees have become more accessible
- with people working for another business or with customers – this is **external contact** – great care is needed when calling because the person involved could be anywhere if the call is not expected, at work, at home, in the shower; this is where business contact can become a nuisance and business etiquette can 'go out of the window'

PHONE ETIQUETTE

the need for phone etiquette

The increasing use of the phone for business communications means that:

- people working **away from the office** will increasingly find themselves in places and situations where it may be awkward or rude to make or receive calls on a mobile phone, for example in a restaurant, in a meeting or in a 'quiet' carriage on a train
- people working **in the office** will also find themselves in situations where it may be awkward or rude to use a mobile or landline phone where they might distract other people's work, or when they are in meetings or when a colleague is on an important call

It is important therefore that people working in business should learn:

- when it **is** appropriate to use a mobile (or landline) phone for business communications
- when it **is not** appropriate to use a mobile (or landline) phone for business communications

People working in business should appreciate that **phone etiquette** is based on the need to present a **professional and polite image** to other businesses and to customers. It also means that they should have respect for their colleagues, both in terms of the language they use and also because making phone calls in the office can be disruptive and disturb other people.

On the next page are some guidelines for business etiquette. Study these and then read the Case Study that follows.

tips on phone etiquette – general rules

The following tips on using the telephone should be followed by people working in any business:

- assuming that you are not using a video link remember that the person on the other end of the phone can only listen to you and cannot see your expressions or your body language – you should speak clearly, slowly and in a polite, professional tone of voice
- do not speak too loudly – the person you are speaking to may be hundreds of miles away, but you do not have to bear this in mind when talking to them
- do not eat or drink when you are dealing with a call – it does not give a professional image of your business if the person at the other end can hear you eating an apple, munching crisps or slurping coffee
- do not use slang or language that is too casual
- never use swear words or make politically incorrect remarks
- address the other person using his or her family name, unless you know the person well – never address somebody you do not know by his or her first name
- if you are on a call and taking down information such as an email address or a string of numbers, it is always a good idea to repeat the information back to the other person to confirm that you have got it right
- never 'lose your cool' – if someone shouts at you on the phone, listen to what they have to say and be polite – never shout back or be rude, however much you feel like throwing the phone at them

maintaining confidentiality

'Maintaining confidentiality' in business means knowing when you should and when you should **not** disclose information about the business you work for to people outside the business. When using the telephone you should:

- never give away confidential information about your business – this can include financial information, details of your colleagues (eg people calling and asking for their personal phone numbers), and details of dealings with other businesses, eg customers
- be aware of people around you and be careful what you say – someone next to you might overhear confidential information which they should not know about and then pass it on to people outside the business
- never give away confidential information about your business when leaving messages on voicemail – anyone with access to the phone could pick up the message

telephone guidelines set down by a business

The 'tips' on the previous page give general guidance to professional behaviour which should be adopted within any business. There are circumstances, however, where the business may set down specific **policies and procedures** for using a telephone – and here we mean both the main landline and private and business mobile phones. Here are some examples:

Policies and Procedures: telephone usage at work

1 Making and receiving phone calls through the main switchboard is for exclusive use by employees solely in connection with the company's business.

2 The company will allow essential 'emergency' personal telephone calls concerning an employee's domestic arrangements, but use of the telephone for personal calls is prohibited.

3 Personal mobile phones cannot be used in company time except during normal breaks.

4 Employees should not allow mobile phones to disturb others in the company's offices; they should keep phones on 'silent' at all times so that loud ring tones – such as bells, heavy metal and animal noises – will not disturb other employees.

You will see from this that using the telephone at work in a professional way and treating people with consideration applies just as much to colleagues as it does to outsiders.

telephone 'scripts' used in business

You will no doubt be aware of the nuisance telephone calls that people get from companies selling products they do not want or need. These calls follow a set 'script' and normally go along the lines of:

'Good morning'	(your reply is 'good morning')
'And how are you today?'	(your thoughts are 'feeling pretty fed up with sales calls, actually')

These callers work from a set script which can make the caller sound parrot-like and insincere. This is obviously an example of a bad use of a scripted call, but the clear message here is that if employees are asked to work from a set script they should:

- sound natural and as if they are really interested in what they are saying
- be able to judge the reaction of the person they have called by their tone of voice and what they say in reply; they should then adapt their tone of voice accordingly and only proceed with the call if they think they are getting somewhere
- thank the person called for their time

On the pages that follow are two Case Studies illustrating how telephone etiquette should be used and sometimes is not used.

The first Case Study is set in a letting agency business that rents out houses and flats.

Case Study

JAVIER PEREZ – TELEPHONE ETIQUETTE

situation

Javier Perez works as a sales assistant at Portmain Lettings, a business that rents residential properties. He shares an office with three other sales assistants who all deal with telephone enquiries and customers who walk in off the street.

It is 11.30am and all of Javier's colleagues are at their desks busy dealing with customers. Javier has just made a coffee when his mobile phone rings with a number that he doesn't recognise. Javier answers it and the following conversation occurs.

Javier: 'Hello, Javier Perez speaking.'

Caller: 'Hello, Javier. This is Simon Stephenson from HT Recruitment. I'm calling about a possible job opportunity you might be interested in.'

Javier does not recognise the name.

Javier: 'I'm not really looking to move jobs at the moment.'

Simon: 'Can I ask what salary you are currently paid at Portmain Lettings and we can see if this other job will pay more?'

Javier: 'Well my basic salary is £11,000 per year but I get a 5% commission on all lettings I arrange. Other members of the team who have been here longer get £17,000 plus commission.'

Javier then takes a slurp of his coffee.

Simon: 'The opportunity I have for you pays £16,000 basic with 5% commission and you get a company car thrown in.'

Javier splutters over his coffee and before he can stop himself exclaims loudly in surprise.

Javier: 'Holy Moly!'

Simon: 'I thought that might get your attention! If you are interested you can come over to my office this evening after work and we can talk some more.'

Javier: 'Sounds good, mate! I can be there at 5.30. What's the address?

Simon: 'Have you got a pen?'

Javier: 'Nah, mate I'll be fine. I'll remember it.'

Simon: 'We're at 64A Brightman Street. If you want to park you'll have to come round to the back of the building. The code for the car park is 3452. Once you get to the door the code to get in is #2391. We're on the third floor.'

Javier: 'Great – see you then.'

identifying the problems

What issues does this situation raise in relation to Javier's telephone etiquette and how should he have dealt with the situation?

solution

- Generally personal calls should not be made or received on work phone lines or personal mobiles during working hours. As Javier does not recognise the telephone number he should not have taken the call. If it is important the caller will leave a message and Javier can call back during his lunch break or after work.

- Having answered his phone and realising that it is a personal call Javier should either ask Simon to call back later, or offer to call him during his lunch break.

- Javier should not provide Simon with his own salary details or those of his colleagues. This is confidential information that should not be shared with somebody outside the business. Also, he is in an open office space with public access and colleagues and customers can hear what he is saying.

- Javier should not be drinking coffee when he is on the phone.

- Javier should not use language such as 'Holy Moly' on the phone or exclaim loudly. Firstly this is inappropriate telephone etiquette shown to the caller and secondly there are colleagues and customers in the office who might hear him.

- Javier calls Simon 'mate'. This is the first conversation Javier has had with Simon and although the call is not directly work-related he is in the office and so should use professional language rather than this casual greeting.

- Javier should have written down the information about how to get to Simon's office and should then have repeated it back to him to confirm the details.

The second Case Study illustrates the dangers of asking employees to read from a fixed 'script' when making sales calls, and especially 'cold calls' to people not known by the business. As you will see, if this process is used insensitively, it can break many of the rules of telephone etiquette.

Case Study

ERIKA – THE DANGERS OF KEEPING TO A SCRIPT

situation

Erika has recently been employed as a telesales assistant at Wonderful Windows, a national double-glazing windows company. The supervisor is currently on holiday and the manager of her department has shown her to her desk and given her a telephone script saying; 'Erika, your supervisor will be back on Monday. She will train you up but in the meantime we're really busy so you can help out with making some of these calls. Make sure you stick to the script. If you have any problems just ask one of the others.'

Erika dials the first telephone number, which is for Mr Henry Foot. The following conversation takes place.

Henry Foot: 'Hello?'

Erika: 'Hello. Please may I speak to Mr Henry Boot?'

Henry Foot: 'My name is Henry Foot, not Henry Boot.'

Erika: 'Hello Henry, how are you today?'

Henry Foot: 'Actually, I'm very busy. Who is calling please?'

Erika: 'Do you have double-glazing in your house?'

Henry Foot: 'Yes, but..........'

Erika *(interrupts):*

'I'm calling from Wonderful Windows and I have a great offer for you. At the moment we are offering all new customers a free no obligation quote for replacement windows. What time of the day is convenient for one of our estimators to visit?'

Henry Foot: 'We only replaced our windows two years ago so I'm not interested in a quote.'

Erika: 'There is no obligation on your part to go ahead with the replacement and if you find a better price on the market we will match it.'

Henry Foot: 'I'm afraid you are not listening to me. I do not want a quote as I had my windows replaced two years ago. Please remove my telephone number from your records and do not call me again.'

Erika: 'Okay, if you're not interested at the moment I'll add you to our list for a call back in six months' time. Thank you for your time. Good-bye.'

identifying the problems

What etiquette problems does sticking to a set script cause Erika when she calls Mr Foot? How could Erika have improved the call?

solution

Some of the problems with Erika's telephone etiquette occur because she is using a script and has not had any training from her supervisor. For example:

- Erika asks to speak to Henry when his name is actually Henry Foot. Before making a business telephone call it is essential that you have accurate information – using the correct name of the person you are calling is very important.

- Once she has confirmed his name Erika uses Henry Foot's first name rather than 'Mr Foot'. As she does not know Henry Foot and he has not told her to call him by his first name Erika should call him Mr Foot rather than Henry.

- Henry Foot says that he is very busy but Erika does not take any notice of this and carries on with the telephone script. Erika should have apologised for bothering him and explained that the call would not take very long, or alternatively she should have asked whether there was a more convenient time to call back when he was less busy.

- As soon as Henry Foot confirms that he has double-glazing Erika interrupts even though he is trying to tell her that the windows are new. Erika should have let Henry Foot complete his sentence as interrupting is very rude and highlights the fact that Erika is reading from a script.

- Erika makes the offer of a visit and a free 'no obligation quote' and then tries to schedule an appointment without giving Henry Foot the chance to say whether he is even interested in a quote. Before offering to arrange a visit Erika should have first confirmed with Henry Foot that he was interested in receiving a quote.

- Henry Foot says that he is not interested in a quote but Erika continues with the offer of a price guarantee. Erika should not ignore what Henry has said. Once he has said that he is not interested she should politely thank him for his time and end the call.

- Finally, Erika realises that Henry Foot is not interested in a quote. However, even though he says that he does not want Wonderful Windows to call again, Erika says that she will schedule a call back for six months later. Erika should not have said this as Henry Foot has specifically asked her to remove his number from Wonderful Windows' records. She should have thanked him for his time and confirmed that he will not receive any further calls from Wonderful Windows.

Chapter Summary

- The use of the telephone in business has greatly increased in recent years, and this has impacted on the way in which business is carried out and also where it is carried out.
- The main area of growth in telephone usage is the mobile phone, which now enables business to be carried out, not only in the office but also outside the office, including on the road and in the home.
- As with many forms of business communication, use of the phone can be internal (within the business) or external (with other businesses or customers).
- Adopting a polite and professional telephone etiquette is very important when dealing not only with external calls, but also with internal communications.
- Maintaining confidentiality when using the telephone is an important principle of professional, ethical behaviour and relates to dealing not only with outsiders but also your own colleagues.
- Businesses may set down guidelines (Policies and Procedures) for the use of the telephone by employees in the workplace, for example covering the making of private calls.
- Businesses can also use 'scripted' calls for standard telephone communications (eg sales calls); these should be used sensitively and avoid sounding as if they are scripted calls.

Key Terms

mobile twinning — using the same phone number to contact someone on both a landline and a mobile phone

phone etiquette — presenting a professional and polite image of your business when communicating by phone

confidentiality — knowing when you should and when you should not disclose information about your business to people outside your business

Policies and Procedures — rules established within a business covering various areas of the operation of the business, eg phone usage

telephone 'scripts' — a fixed text provided to people making phone calls on behalf of the business, eg sales calls

Activities

4.1 Decide which of the following is the best description of 'mobile twinning.' Tick the option you choose.

		✔
(a)	A call plan in which calls to certain phone numbers are cheaper or free	
(b)	Having more than one mobile phone with the same telephone number	
(c)	Using the same phone number to contact someone on both a landline and a mobile phone	
(d)	Buying two mobile phones for the price of one	

4.2 Consider each of the following statements and decide whether it is true or false. Tick either true or false for each one.

	True ✔	**False** ✔
It is acceptable to make a personal call on the work phone line provided you are not very busy.		
Personal mobile phones should be kept on silent mode during office hours.		
If you know the person you are contacting is busy it is more appropriate to phone them rather than send an email.		
It is acceptable to discuss confidential information on the phone in a large office where lots of people work.		
When using a telephone script it is important to stick to the precise words regardless of the answers from the customer.		
When travelling on a train it is better to text or email a colleague rather than having a mobile phone conversation.		

4.3 Read through the following situation and then carry out the task below.

Kate Boyd works as a personal trainer. She is employed on a part-time basis five mornings a week at the Jimmie Floyd Health Club. She also offers individual one-to-one sessions on a self-employed basis.

It is 10.25 and Kate is about to teach a class at 10.30. Most of the people who are booked in for the class are already in the studio when Kate's mobile phone rings. She recognises the number as that of one of her regular personal training clients. She answers the call. The following conversation occurs.

Kate: 'Hello, Ryan. How are things?'

Ryan: 'Hi Kate. All's well with me thanks. I was wondering if we could arrange another session for next week?'

The mobile phone reception in parts of the Jimmie Floyd Health Club is poor and Kate is struggling to hear what Ryan is saying in the studio where her class is now gathering. She decides that the best solution is to speak in a very loud voice:

Kate: 'Yes that should be fine. I'll have to get my diary and check when I'm free.'

Kate walks out of the studio where the 10.30 class is due to take place and goes to the office down the corridor to get her diary. On her way back to the studio she continues the phone conversation with Ryan:

Kate: 'Right! When were you thinking of?'

Ryan: 'Do you have any slots for Tuesday afternoon after 3.30pm? I'm very keen to work off some of this weight before I go on holiday next month.'

By now Kate has walked back to the studio where the phone reception is poor and again has to speak in a very loud voice:

Kate: 'Yes Ryan we'll need to work on that tummy before you put on those swimming trunks! How about 4pm on Tuesday?'

Ryan: 'Great, see you then.'

Kate ends the call at 10.38am.

You are to:

Identify and describe all the instances where Kate is not complying with telephone etiquette. Suggest in each case how Kate should have dealt with the call in a professional way.

5 Business meetings

this chapter covers...

A meeting is a form of business communication which requires personal skills and a knowledge of format and documentation. This chapter covers the areas of:

- *why meetings are needed*
- *different types of meeting – internal/external, formal and informal*
- *face-to-face meetings and online conferencing*
- *meetings for different purposes within an organisation*
- *the documents needed for meetings and reasons for using them*
- *the personal skills needed for taking an effective part in a meeting:*
  - *being able to listen to a discussion*
  - *being able to contribute to a discussion*

THE NEED FOR MEETINGS

why have meetings?

Meetings are an important form of communication as they make it possible for organisations to:

- **inform people** – eg introducing a new product, explaining redundancies
- **make plans** – eg staff planning, product planning
- **sort out problems** – eg facing price cuts by competitors, staff parking
- **make decisions** – eg whether to drop an out-of-date product, or to export

In this chapter we will concentrate on **business meetings**, although there are other types of organisation which regularly hold meetings, for example:

- local authorities
- sports clubs
- charities
- the Government

The issues discussed at meetings of these non-business organisations may be different, but the advantages to these organisations of holding meetings will be the same: informing, planning, resolving problems and making decisions.

classification of business meetings

There are many different ways in which meetings can be held. They can be:

- **internal** – in other words, taking place within a single business
- **external** – meeting with people outside the business, either an individual (eg an accountant) or with another organisation (eg a supplier, the bank, a company customer)

Meetings can also be:

- **informal** – meetings which may be unscheduled, with a friend in the business, or a confidential meeting – these may be undocumented
- **formal** – meetings which are scheduled, documented and known about by the people in the business or businesses involved

USING INFORMATION TECHNOLOGY IN MEETINGS

face-to-face meetings

The traditional form of business meeting is a **face-to-face meeting** where people sit around a table in the same room and carry on the business of the meeting – making presentations, answering questions, discussing issues and making decisions. Communication in this case is natural, relying on facial expressions, body language and tone of voice.

online meetings - Web conferencing

Modern information technology is now making changes to the way meetings are conducted by making it possible for people to communicate when they are in a number of different locations.

This technology is widely known as **Web conferencing** – a form of real-time communication (RTC) in which a number of computer users share online video, audio and text-based communications, each seeing the same screen through their Web browsers. Web conferencing allows any number of people to join meetings and these people can be anywhere in the world, as can be seen in the diagram below. This shows an international Web conference with users based in a variety of continents.

Web conferencing – online data sharing

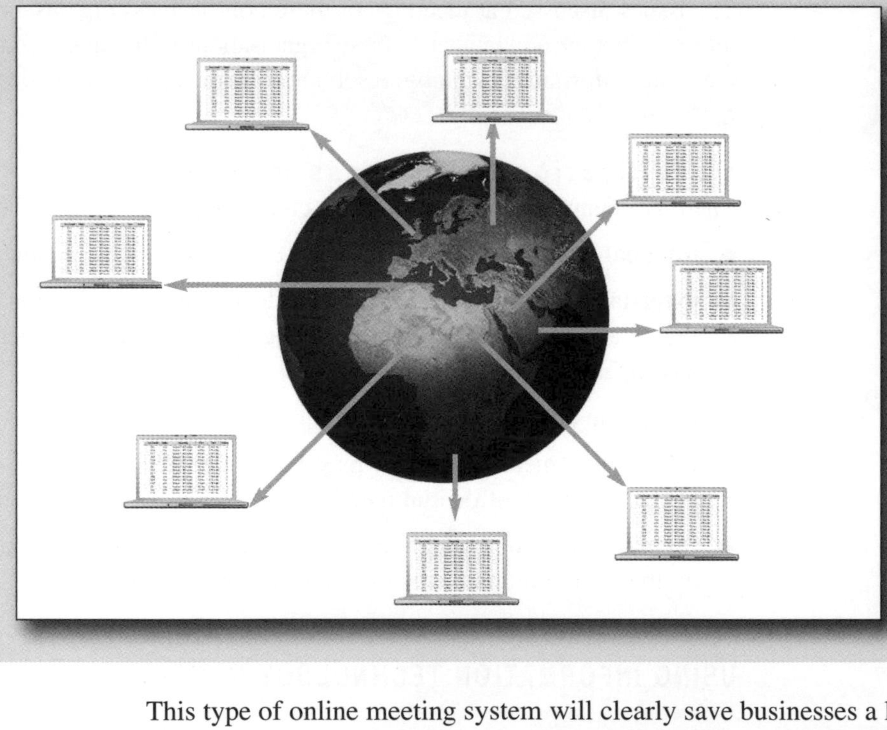

This type of online meeting system will clearly save businesses a lot of time and money, but an online meeting may not always allow the high level of personal communication that a true face-to-face meeting will provide. Study the picture at the top of the next page to see how effective a face-to-face meeting can be.

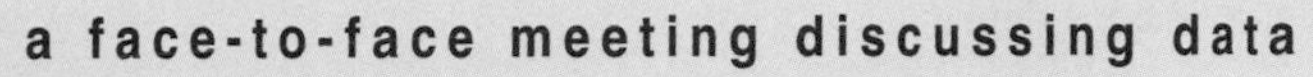
a face-to-face meeting discussing data

© Getty Images

using the phone and internet to include extra people

It is possible that a meeting may be held but certain important people are unable to get to it. In this case it is useful to be able to set up links so that these 'missing' people can join in the discussions. This can be achieved using a telephone with a 'speaker' or, better still, by creating an online link using video communication which turns the meeting into a mix of face-to-face and Web conferencing. An example of an online video linked meeting is shown in the picture below.

a face-to-face meeting using an online video link

© Getty Images

TYPES OF MEETING

Business meetings are held for a number of different purposes and with varying numbers of people. Here are some examples:

- **departmental meetings** – these are **formal meetings** in which all the staff in an individual department within a business (eg Sales Department, Accounts Department) get together on a regular basis to report and discuss various issues. These issues might include:
  - how the department is performing – has it met its targets?
  - how the department could improve its performance
  - plans for the future – a new sales campaign, improved financial reporting
  - operational problems, eg phone communication, document checking
  - housekeeping, eg recycling of paper, the coffee machine, fire alarms
  - external events, eg parties, team-building trips, charity runs

- **team meetings** – these are formal specialist meetings in which individuals dealing with specific functions in the business get together on a regular basis to monitor current activity and to plan ahead. These could include:
  - special project developments, eg a new computer network system
  - Health & Safety in the workplace

  The team members may all be from the same department or, more likely, they may be drawn from different departments.

- **staff appraisal meetings** – these are held regularly in most businesses and are 'one-to-one' work progress assessments of an individual member of staff by a manager. The issues discussed will normally include a formal assessment of the employee by the manager, feedback from the employee and plans for job progression and extra training.

You can see from this wide range of meetings that:

- meetings can be small (from two upwards) or much larger
- most meetings are held to assess current activity and to plan ahead

It also follows that:

- formal meetings need to be carefully documented so that people can be sure what topics have been covered and what has been decided
- people involved in meetings need to acquire good communication skills

These last two important topics are covered in the rest of this chapter.

the need for a 'chairperson' for a formal meeting

Someone needs to be in strict control of the meeting, otherwise it may ramble on, not cover all the agenda, and possibly be dominated by people who have an 'issue' and like the sound of their own voice.

It is normal practice for a formal meeting, eg a departmental meeting, to appoint a **chairperson**. In the case of a departmental meeting the chairperson is likely to be the departmental manager.

The duties of a chairperson are to:

- sign the minutes of the previous meeting when the members now present have agreed that they accurately reflect what was said and decided in the earlier meeting
- lead and control the meeting
- summarise and clarify decisions so that they can be minuted
- decide when to move on to the next agenda item

action list

It is useful if the person writing out the minutes ends with a list of '**actions**' – this will be a list of the people who have to take action as a result of the meeting, together with a summary of what they have to do.

For example:

MG *Investigate possible upgrades to the Sage computer accounting system and send details to MF by Feb 14th*

RT *Identify customer accounts which are over their limit and overdue and send out chaser Letter 4*

Note: the letters 'MG' and 'RT' at the beginning of each action are the initials of the person who has to carry out that action.

An action list is useful in two ways:

- it is a prompt to the relevant person to get on with what is required
- if there is any question later on about who was responsible for doing the task, it is set out in the minutes in writing and cannot be argued with

It is useful to send the minutes to anyone who could not come to the meeting:

- to provide information about what was covered and decided at the meeting
- to make sure that the person not present at the meeting carries out any task(s) allocated to them and summarised in the action list

THE SKILLS NEEDED FOR BUSINESS MEETINGS

The two most important communication skills needed for successful participation in meetings are:

- **listening** to what people say
- **speaking** – ie making appropriate contributions to the discussion

listening skills

You need to listen carefully when you are taking part in a meeting. Unless you take in and understand what is being said you will not be in a position to speak at the meeting and argue a point. Listening involves three main stages:

- **hearing** – this means taking in what is said so that it enters your short-term memory as a fact, for example:

  'Over 20% of our customers do not pay up on time.'

- **understanding** – this means that you can identify that there is a problem, in this case that customers are poor payers, leading you to think:

  'This is not good! What are we going to do about it?'

- **decision making** – this means that you can make suggestions in the meeting which might help solve the problem:

  'Can we charge them interest on what they owe after the date for payment stated on the invoice?'

This brings us to the second skill you will need to develop: making a contribution to the meeting.

contributing at a meeting

As you may know from watching TV programmes such as 'The Apprentice', some people talk more than others in meetings. The non-contributor finds it easier to sit back and let the mind wander or look at a mobile phone under the table during a meeting. This behaviour is of no use to the business. At the other extreme some people are all 'mouth' and talk too much, sometimes talking total rubbish. This behaviour can be disruptive in a meeting and it will be up to the chairperson to keep that person under control.

What makes an effective contributor? An effective contributor at a meeting should, as seen above, **listen** and take in what people say and **understand** the situation. If it is a problem that is being discussed, a suggestion for solving the problem could be made. But of course not every point made at a meeting represents a problem. The effective contributor at a meeting could also:

- **ask a question** if the subject needs more explanation
- **agree with someone** if the point they make is important – and then make another point which supports what they have said
- **disagree** if the information given or a solution suggested seems to be wrong
- **provide information and feedback** if asked to do so, either at the meeting itself or as a response to an item on the agenda, for example:

  'Over 20% of our customers do not pay up on time.'

Bear in mind that it is always the effective contributors at a meeting that people remember and not the quiet and timid ones who say nothing.

Also note that you should always be helpful and courteous in meetings and not argumentative or aggressive, however you may feel at the time.

We will now look at a Case Study in which a meeting goes wrong.

Case Study

BENBOY MUSIC – CARLA'S PROBLEM MEETING

situation

Carla James is Finance Manager at Benboy Music, a record label that produces a number of successful bands and solo artists. The Accounts Department is located in a large office complex on the outskirts of London which is also where the recording studio is based. It is not unusual to see some very famous music stars coming in and out of the building. The Accounts Department holds a monthly team meeting that all 15 members of staff are expected to attend. An email with the agenda for the June meeting (see below) is sent by Carla at 4.45pm on Wednesday 7 June; the meeting is scheduled for 10.30am on Thursday 8 June.

Accounts Department monthly meeting

Date 7 June 20XX
Time 10.30am
Venue 3rd Floor Meeting Room C

Agenda

1 Apologies
2 Minutes of previous meeting
3 Manager's report
4 Artist expense claims
5 Report on the upgrade of computer accounting system
6 Any other business
7 Date and time of the next meeting

On Thursday, the day of the meeting, Carla and the accounts team arrive at Meeting Room C promptly at 10.30am. Johnnie Evans, the Finance Director, normally chairs the meeting but is not attending, so the Finance Manager, Carla James, is chairperson.

Carla checks that everyone has a copy of the agenda and the meeting starts. The following events occur during the meeting:

Item 1 Apologies

Apologies have been received from Johnnie Evans and two other members of the team.

Item 2 Minutes of previous meeting

Carla moves on to approval of minutes for the previous meeting, but no one has a copy of the minutes and it soon becomes clear that they were not sent out with the agenda, as they would normally be. Carla decides not to worry about this and drops item 2 from the agenda.

Item 3 Manager's report

Carla then hands out copies of her monthly report and runs through the key points. There is a detailed discussion about the increased time it is taking to collect money from customers and the meeting then moves on to item 4 on the agenda.

Item 4 Artist expense claims

Carla explains that there have been some serious issues regarding the expenses incurred by several of their star singers and bands. She is keen to implement a stricter control over what they are and are not allowed to spend. Ravi, one of the new accounts assistants asks if he might make a point. He then says that he thinks all artists should be allowed to 'spend what they like' as they are such big stars. He proceeds to talk about how exciting it is to work in the same building as his favourite recording artists, how he sees many of them in the lift and how nice they all are. Nothing of what Ravi says is relevant to the issue and after ten minutes of non-stop talking, several other members of the team start looking at their watches and then at Carla.

Carla does nothing to stop Ravi and although a number of her colleagues make some valid points, he continues to dominate the conversation.

Before moving on to point 5 on the agenda, Carla asks: 'did we get all that down in the minutes?' Everyone looks blankly at her and she realises that no one has been asked to take the minutes. She then asks Antonia, an Accounts Assistant, to take the minutes.

Item 5 Upgrade of the computer accounting system

Carla turns to Rhys Davies and says: 'Right, item 5 on the agenda. Over to you Rhys.' Rhys looks confused. After some discussion it appears that Rhys was not at the previous meeting when he was

asked to produce a report on the upgrade to the computer accounting system. As the action plan from that meeting was never circulated, Rhys was not aware of this and so has not prepared anything. Carla decides that this item will have to be postponed to the next meeting and that the minutes should reflect this as an action point for Rhys. Rhys points out that this means he will be reporting after the upgrades have 'gone live', so there will be no opportunity to change anything by that stage.

Item 6 **Any other business**

The meeting drags on until 12.15pm when Carla suddenly exclaims: 'Oh heck! I have another meeting at 12.30 and I need to grab a sandwich!' She winds up the meeting saying: ' if anyone has AOB – any other business – please email it to Antonia or save it until the next meeting. Sorry – got to run!'

Item 7 **Date and time of the next meeting**

Everyone heads off but no date or time is agreed for the next meeting.

What has gone wrong with this meeting?
What are the possible consequences?
Could things have been done better?

- The minutes from the previous meeting have not been circulated and so cannot be approved at this meeting. Consequently, there may be errors in the minutes that may go unnoticed. There may also be action points that have been allocated but not actioned.

- Ravi takes up a large amount of time at the meeting talking about unrelated issues and monopolising the conversation. This could have several possible consequences. Other people at the meeting may get annoyed that Ravi has been able to dominate the discussion and they may 'switch off'. This could mean that they do not contribute relevant points to the discussion. It could also mean that there is insufficient time to discuss items that appear later in the agenda. Carla should have taken control of this situation, allowing others to voice their opinions and then moving on to the next agenda item at an appropriate time.

- Carla has forgotten to appoint someone to take the minutes. By the time she realises this and asks Antonia to do it, several important points have been discussed. This could result in key issues being left out of the minutes and people being unaware of action points for which they are responsible.

- The minutes and the action plan from the previous meeting have not been circulated and consequently Rhys did not know he was expected to report on the system upgrade. This means that he will have no opportunity to report to the meeting and address any concerns raised before the upgrade is implemented.

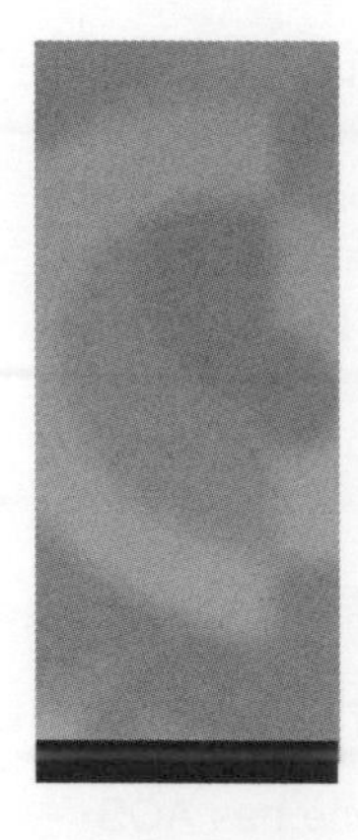

- The meeting has overrun due to Carla's lack of leadership and control as chairperson. The consequence of this is that there has not been time for item 6 on the agenda – any other business. This is the part of the meeting where people have the opportunity to raise any issues that are not on the agenda and can often be when urgent or important matters are raised. Suggesting that any other business is postponed until the next meeting may mean that important issues are not discussed and addressed.
- No date and time for the next meeting were set. It is better to arrange the next meeting at the end of the current meeting to ensure that it is entered into people's diaries. Circulating these arrangements at a later date runs the risk that people cannot attend.

Chapter Summary

- Meetings are an important form of communication for many types of organisation and their main functions are to inform, plan, sort problems and make decisions.
- Meetings can be internal or external, formal or informal, face-to-face or online.
- Types of meeting include departmental meetings, team meetings and staff appraisals.
- Formal meetings need to be carefully documented in the form of an agenda and minutes. A chairperson is also needed to manage a formal meeting.
- An action list for people to take on tasks discussed at the meeting will be issued after the meeting; this should be circulated to the people who came or were invited to the meeting.
- Listening skills and the ability to contribute to discussion are needed in order to make meetings effective and the organisation function well.

Key Terms

internal meeting	a meeting held by staff within a business
external meeting	a meeting also involving people outside the business
formal meeting	a meeting which is scheduled and documented, often involving a large group of people
informal meeting	a meeting held on a more relaxed basis, normally between individuals; these meetings may not necessarily be documented
departmental meeting	a regular formal meeting involving employees within an individual department of a business
team meeting	a meeting held for a special purpose involving employees who may be from different departments
web conferencing	online conferencing using video and audio links enabling people in different locations to hold meetings
agenda	a list of items to be covered in a formal meeting sent out in advance to the people attending
minutes	a written record of items discussed and decisions made at a formal meeting; they should be approved at the following meeting and signed by the chairperson
chairperson	the person who directs and manages a formal meeting; one of his/her duties is to sign the previous meeting's minutes when they have been approved by the people at the current meeting
action list	a written list of actions decided upon in the meeting, recorded in the minutes and assigned to different individuals
listening skills	skills important in meetings, involving the processes of hearing what is said, understanding it and deciding what (if anything) to say in the meeting
contributor	a person who takes an active part in a meeting, making suggestions, providing information, giving feedback, asking questions, agreeing and disagreeing as appropriate with points that are made in the meeting

Activities

5.1 Complete the following statements about business meetings by selecting the appropriate words from the list shown below (not all words will be needed).

The .... is the document that states what needs to be covered in a meeting.

All items discussed at the meeting are recorded in the ....

The meeting is controlled by the .... who will normally be someone senior attending the meeting.

Extra items that were not originally scheduled for discussion at a meeting can be covered in ....

It is important to confirm the .... of the next meeting during the current meeting.

agenda **date and time** **any other business**

apologies **minutes** **chairperson**

5.2 'If you are a junior member of staff at a meeting it is generally not appropriate to contribute to a discussion point, as your role at the meeting should always be to listen and learn.'

State whether the statement above is true or false. Tick the appropriate box.

	✔
True	
False	

5.3 Which of the following best describes a scheduled meeting between your Accounts Supervisor and the Sales Manager of a supplier company. Minutes will be taken at the meeting.

		✔
(a)	Internal and informal	
(b)	Internal and formal	
(c)	External and informal	
(d)	External and formal	

5.4 Ishmael is a Customer Services Assistant at Bluebay Ltd. He is very concerned about the way in which certain members of the team are handling customer enquiries. He plans to raise this at the next monthly team meeting. The Customer Services Supervisor has already prepared the agenda for this meeting. Answer all of the questions set out below.

(a) State which item on a meeting agenda will give Ishmael the opportunity to raise this issue.

(b) Describe how the minutes of the previous month's meeting should be dealt with at the next meeting and who is responsible for this.

(c) Ishmael is planning to use specific examples of what he believes to be poor customer service from some of his colleagues who will be present at the meeting.

Explain whether or not it is appropriate for Ishmael to do this.

(d) Explain why it is a good idea to arrange the date and time of the next meeting at the end of the current meeting.

5.5 The Accounts Department at Supreme Insurance holds a monthly departmental meeting at which all eight members of the team have the opportunity to discuss any issues that have arisen.

It is 9.45am and this month's meeting is due to start at 10am. A reminder of the time and location of the meeting was sent out by email the day before but there was no agenda attached to it.

The following events occurred at the meeting.

1. Seth Cunningham, the Accounts Manager, chairs the meeting. He appoints Sara Gough to take the minutes. Sara is a trainee who joined the business two weeks ago straight from school. She has never attended a team meeting before.
2. Seth distributes copies of the agenda to the team and apologises for it being late.

Accounts Department monthly meeting

Date 18 August 20XX

Time 10.30am

Venue Meeting Room 4.2

Agenda

1 Apologies

2 Manager's report

3 Arrangements for staff appraisals

4 Update on the Accounts Department's move to the second floor

5 Any other business

6 Date and time of the next meeting

3. Apologies have been received from three people who are unable to attend the meeting.

4. Simon, one of the Supervisors, points out that normally item 2 on the agenda is 'Minutes of the previous meeting' but that no one had received these. Seth explains that he has forgotten to distribute them but there was nothing important to raise and he would sign them off after the meeting.

5. Seth deals with his Manager's report, which does not raise any major issues.

6. The discussion about the arrangements for staff appraisals was detailed but straightforward, with all members of staff confirming that they understood the process and their responsibilities.

   At the end of this discussion Seth commented that all the details would be included in the meeting minutes, glancing at Sara as he said it. Sara looked very worried.

7. Seth turns to Michaela Fogarty and says, 'Right Michaela. Over to you for item 4.'

   Michaela looks at him blankly.

   It turns out that she was not present at the previous meeting when she was asked to provide a detailed update on the Accounts Department's move to the second floor, which is due to take place at the end of August.

   Michaela is unable to provide this information, so Seth decides to move on to 'Any Other Business'.

8. Arthur Bennett asks if he can raise an issue.

   He then proceeds to explain in great detail how dissatisfied he is with the quality of the food in the staff restaurant. In particular he does not like the sausages that they serve, saying that they appear to be poor quality. Arthur is known for 'liking the sound of his own voice.' No one joins in the conversation and after five minutes Arthur finishes speaking and the meeting moves on to the next point.

9. It is agreed that the next meeting will take place on 16 September at the same time.

10. At the end of the meeting Seth calls Sara over and says:

    'I hope you got all that down. If you can write up the minutes and distribute them to the whole team that would be great. Thanks for your help!'

    Sara has written five points on her pad during the meeting, one of which is 'poor quality sausages'. She has no idea how meeting minutes should be prepared.

Answer the following questions about the meeting described above.

(a) Explain the possible consequences of Seth not distributing the previous meeting minutes before this meeting and then removing them from the agenda.

(b) Decide whether it was sensible for Seth to nominate Sara to take the minutes of the meeting. Explain your reasons.

(c) As Michaela was not present at the previous meeting how should she have known that she had been tasked with providing an update on the Accounts Department office move?

(d) State who is responsible for controlling what is raised in the 'Any Other Business' part of the meeting and suggest how Arthur's objections to the catering should have been managed.

6 Personal skills at work

this chapter covers...

Personal skills are skills that enable you to deal with situations in business and also in your private life.

The personal skills which will be particularly useful in the workplace are:

- *time management*
- *showing initiative in what you are doing*
- *showing commitment to what you are doing*
- *being able to persevere in what you are doing*
- *coping with changes in the workplace*

This chapter describes these skills in detail.

The next chapter explains how you can assess your personal and communication skills and make plans to develop them.

WHAT ARE PERSONAL SKILLS?

In this book so far we have described the different types of **communication skills**:

- receiving and sending emails and letters
- using telephones
- organising and taking part in meetings

These skills are very specific and have to be learned and practised.

Personal skills, on the other hand, are very different. They are far more general and relate to:

- your personality
- your ability to deal with people, situations and problems

types of personal skills

Personal skills, as we saw in Chapter 1, include:

- **managing time**, which involves planning ahead and dealing with unexpected events
- **initiative**, which means 'seeing what needs to be done and then getting on and doing it'
- **commitment**, which means 'doing what it takes' and showing loyalty to people and organisations
- **perseverance**, a rather old-fashioned word which means 'sticking at it' or 'keeping going whatever happens'
- **embracing change**, which means 'dealing with and making the most of change', in other words seeing change as a challenge rather than a threat

These five personal skills are not technical skills, such as being able to do double-entry bookkeeping, but are very valuable to people working in an organisation such as a business.

These personal skills can be used not only in business but also as **transferable skills** in your everyday relationships with friends, family or partners. For example, if you are on time for meeting someone for a date, committed in a relationship and able to deal with changes in circumstances (eg you might find out that your date is married), you should be well equipped for dealing with life in general.

The five personal skills listed above are shown in the diagram on the next page. Study this and then read the explanations that follow.

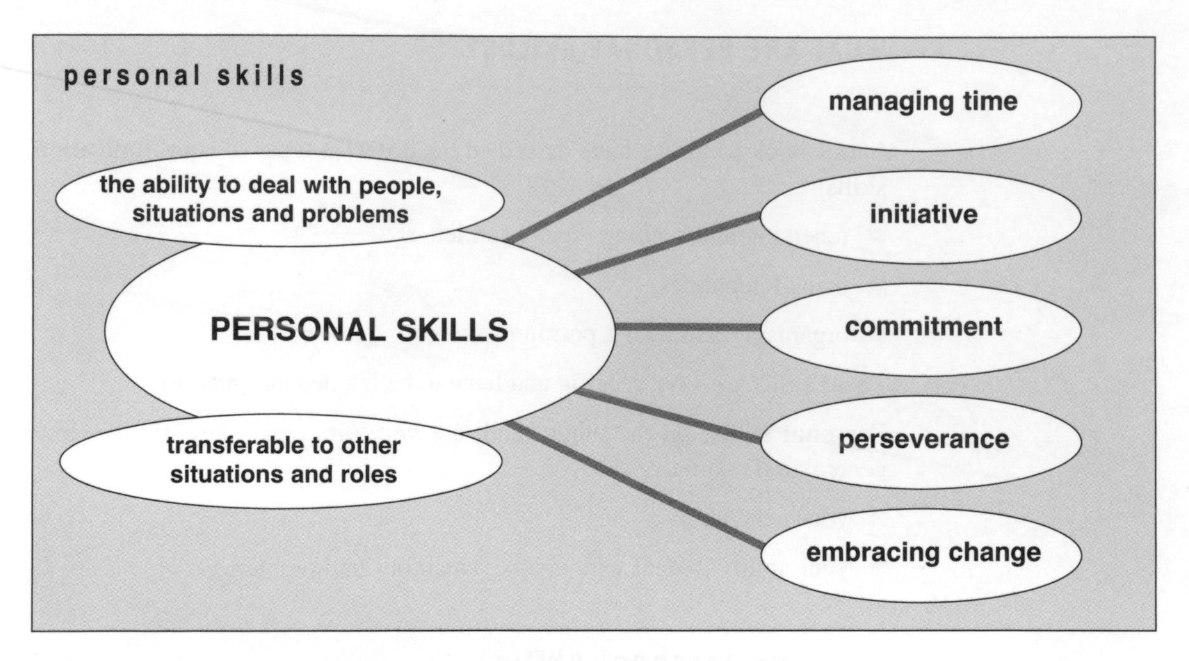

The personal skills shown on the right-hand side of the diagram above can be used in a business in a number of ways.

MANAGING TIME

Managing your time is an important transferable skill at any time of the day, whether you are at work, studying for your exams or cooking a meal at home. Time is very valuable and there is a skill in making the most of it and not wasting it. Time management in the workplace requires you to:

- assess how much time you have available in total
- assess how much time your tasks will take to complete

If you do not have enough time available, you should:

- prioritise your tasks and do the most important tasks first
- if necessary, delegate your work to someone who is willing and has time

If this is not possible tell your manager that you cannot complete all your work – it will then be up to the manager to sort out the problem

Other skills required for effective time management include:

- being punctual and turning up for work and meetings on time
- being decisive and not getting stressed out and achieving nothing if things go wrong
- being flexible and able to change your planned schedule of tasks if the circumstances change

a note on prioritising tasks

Prioritising your tasks – in other words deciding what is the most important task to do – is an important element of time management. There is no use in carrying on making the manager the usual morning cup of coffee if the fire alarm is going off. But the question is – what decides what is the most important task? This not as easy as it may sound.

Prioritising tasks means deciding the order of the tasks. Which one first? Which one last? Which tasks matter? Which tasks do not matter so much? The two main factors involved in the decision are **urgency** and **importance**.

- **urgent tasks**

  These are tasks which have to be done by a deadline that has already arrived or is coming up very soon: a manager needs some sales figures for a meeting that is taking place or customer statements need to be printed to go out in tonight's post.

- **important tasks**

  These are tasks for which you have been given personal responsibility. They may be part of your normal routine and other people depend on them being completed, or they may have been delegated to you because your manager thinks you are capable of completing them.

The table below shows how to work out the order in which you should do tasks, based on the factors of urgency and importance.

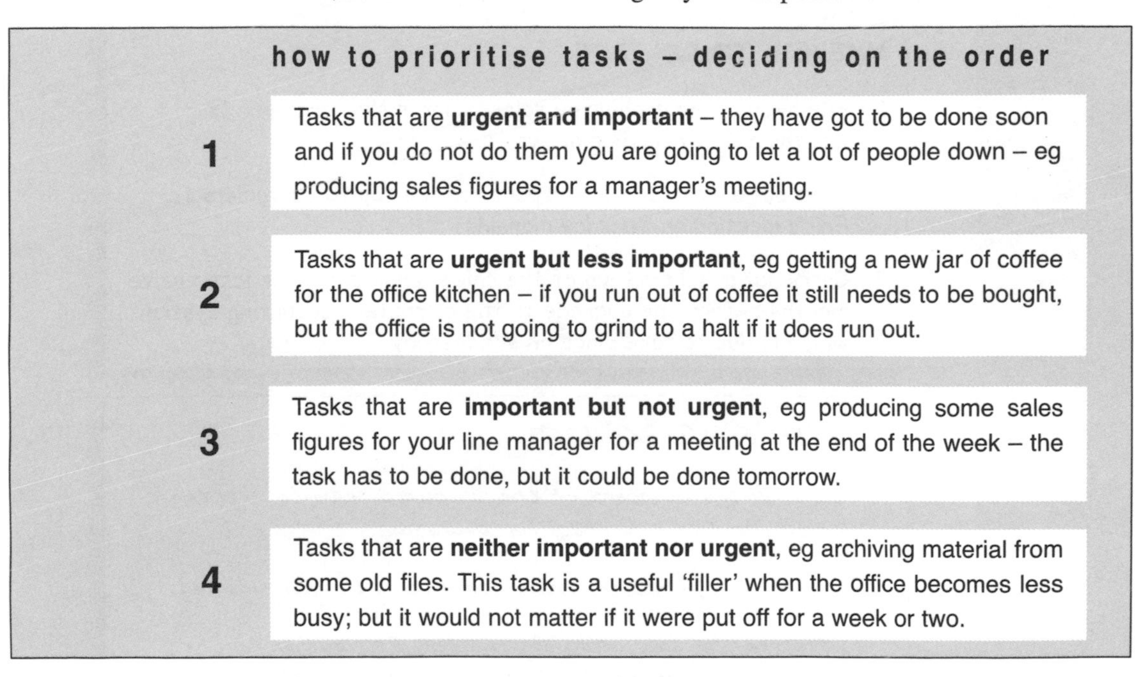

how to prioritise tasks – deciding on the order

1	Tasks that are **urgent and important** – they have got to be done soon and if you do not do them you are going to let a lot of people down – eg producing sales figures for a manager's meeting.
2	Tasks that are **urgent but less important**, eg getting a new jar of coffee for the office kitchen – if you run out of coffee it still needs to be bought, but the office is not going to grind to a halt if it does run out.
3	Tasks that are **important but not urgent**, eg producing some sales figures for your line manager for a meeting at the end of the week – the task has to be done, but it could be done tomorrow.
4	Tasks that are **neither important nor urgent**, eg archiving material from some old files. This task is a useful 'filler' when the office becomes less busy; but it would not matter if it were put off for a week or two.

The Case Study on the next page illustrates the need to develop the personal skill of managing time in the workplace.

Case Study

COOL CLOBBER LTD – MANAGING TIME

situation

Maeve works as a trainee in the Sales Ledger section of the Accounts Department of Cool Clobber Ltd, a large clothing manufacturer.

Normally Maeve shares the routine tasks in the Sales Ledger Section with Daniel the other trainee. These tasks are:

- Checking incoming emails and distributing the post
- Checking sales invoices and credit notes for entry on the computer
- Entering invoices onto the computer system
- Checking entry of data on the computer system

Daniel is on holiday for the whole week and the Line Manager, Eric, has told Maeve that she must cover all their normal routine tasks and also make sure any other important tasks on Daniel's 'to do' list get done.

On Monday morning Maeve is very anxious about how she is going to cope and asks Eric how she should deal with all the tasks she has to do. He tells her to finish the normal daily routine tasks of checking and inputting and to let him know if she runs into any problems. He suggests she then prioritises all the other extra tasks on the 'to do' lists. The two 'to do' lists are shown below:

MAEVE'S 'TO DO' LIST

1 File away in the archive all sales reports that are over 18 months old – when time allows.

2 Print out a monthly sales report for the top 10 customers for Eric's meeting on Tuesday morning.

3 Carry out a full back-up of the sales reports for the last twelve months before the upgrade to the computer accounting system which is due to take place on Wednesday.

DANIEL'S 'TO DO' LIST

1 *Get all ten members of the accounts team to sign the card for Eric's birthday on Wednesday.*

2 *Water the plants in the office – as and when required.*

3 *Prepare the July sales figures for distribution to the company directors for Friday's board meeting.*

solution

Maeve remembers reading in one of her textbooks that when faced with a number of tasks you should prioritise them according to how **urgent** they are and how **important** they are.

Using this method she starts prioritising her own and Daniel's 'to do' lists in the following order, drawing up a new list to work from.

1 **urgent and important tasks**

- Print out a monthly sales report for the top 10 customers for Eric's meeting on Tuesday (tomorrow) morning (Maeve's list)

2 **urgent and less important tasks**

- Get all ten members of the accounts team to sign the card for Eric's birthday on Wednesday (Daniel's list)

3 **important and less urgent tasks**

- Carry out a full back-up of the sales reports for the last twelve months before the upgrade to the computer accounting system planned for Wednesday (Maeve's list)
- Prepare the July sales figures for distribution to the company directors at Friday's board meeting (Daniel's list)

4 **less important and less urgent tasks**

- File away in the archive all sales reports that are over 18 months old (Maeve's list)
- Water the plants in the office if they need it (Daniel's list)

During the week Maeve works through this list of 'to do' items as time and her routine work allows.

She will doubtless also encounter other unexpected tasks and will have to prioritise them as well and fit them into her schedule.

If Maeve gets stuck with planning her work – as she did on Monday morning – she can always ask Eric, her Line Manager, who has overall responsibility for the tasks she does. He will then be able to advise and possibly call in help from other employees if it becomes necessary.

INITIATIVE

A general definition of initiative is:

'assessing and working out what needs to be done and then getting on and making it happen'

starting a new job

Starting a new job is an excellent opportunity for showing that you have initiative. For example you may be given a new job in an accounts office processing sales orders. In your first week you will have to get to know:

- who is who in the office – the manager or supervisor, the experienced staff, the beginners, the people who can help you and those that are not very helpful
- the work itself – the documents involved, using the computer to process sales invoices, the filing systems

You will need **initiative** to get to grips with all these different aspects of office work by using all the resources that are available:

- making the most of training provided, eg formal 'on-the-job' instruction, videos, training manuals, procedures manuals
- interacting with and learning from colleagues doing the same type of work

getting on in a job

As you get used to the job and more experienced you can show initiative by:

- offering to take on new tasks
- suggesting improvements to working methods
- offering to help colleagues who may be struggling to complete their work
- offering to help colleagues who do not understand aspects of their work
- being decisive and offering solutions to problems

In other words you are showing all the qualities of leadership and management which should help you to get promotion – and more money.

The table on the next page illustrates situations where initiative is used and when it is not used.

What you would do in the same situations?

situation	using initiative	not using initiative
You see something that needs improving	You suggest a possible improvement	You put up with the existing situation
You see that a colleague needs help in finishing her work	You offer to help her	You make a comment in the office that she is 'so slow'
You finish your work ahead of time	You look to see if you can help anyone else	You go off and have a coffee and check your Facebook
The fire alarm goes off	You check to see if it is a practice alarm	You wait to see what everyone does
You are in with the manager for your annual appraisal	You suggest going on a course that will help you to get promotion	You say you are very happy with everything except the lack of an afternoon tea break
The manager asks for volunteers for a charity event the business is sponsoring at the weekend	You volunteer your help straightaway as you see it as a way to meet the management socially	You say that you think that you have something else to do at the weekend, but you are not sure

COMMITMENT

Commitment as a personal skill in business means:

'doing what it takes' and showing loyalty to people and the business

Commitment can be demonstrated in a number of ways:

- being willing to carry out all work tasks that you are asked to carry out by an employer, even if they are difficult, challenging or require you to work extra time – this is what 'doing what it takes' means
- 'going the extra mile' to complete a task and to complete it to a high standard
- being willing to carry out work tasks that a colleague asks you to carry out if the colleague is unable to do them or finish them
- being professional in the way that you carry out your work – being punctual, complying with a dress code, putting in extra hours when needed
- being a good team member by contributing well in group tasks and meetings
- showing determination to meet your own personal goals and the goals set in a staff appraisal – for example achieving success on training courses, passing exams and getting a good work grade

Committed employees are very often the employees who are promoted within a business. Committed employees make good leaders and managers.

PERSEVERANCE

Perseverance as a personal skill in business means:

'sticking at it' or 'keeping going whatever happens'

Perseverance can be seen in business:

- when you work hard to complete a difficult task – for example setting up a complex spreadsheet system to provide management reports on the sales performance of a business
- when a task goes horribly wrong because it is not well understood and has to be started again . . . and again . . . and again . . . and is then finally and successfully completed
- when you take professional exams and fail some of them; you then keep working at them and over time eventually pass them all
- when you set both short-term and long-term goals in your job and eventually achieve them through hard work and 'sticking at it'

Case Study

GRADY'S STATIONERY SUPPLIES – INITIATIVE, COMMITMENT AND PERSEVERANCE

situation 1 – Mo

Mo works as a trainee in the Accounts Department of Grady's Stationery Supplies. One of his responsibilities is to file the paper copies of customer orders. A numerical filing system is used with each customer given a unique reference number.

Mo has noticed that with this system you have to look up the customer number in a separate customer list in order to locate the order. Mo decides that this is a total waste of time. He sends an email to all his colleagues asking them if they would find it easier if the orders were filed alphabetically by customer, so avoiding the need to consult a customer list.

All the accounts staff said that they would find it a lot easier. Mo then stayed on after 5pm on the next three days and rearranged all the orders into alphabetical order by customer and relabelled the files to reflect this. He then sent an email to all staff explaining the revised system.

Mo's personal skills – initiative and commitment

Mo has used his **initiative** by identifying the problem with the filing system for customer orders. He has come up with a workable solution and implemented it without being asked to. He has also shown **commitment** to the business by staying late on three days to ensure that the new system is implemented promptly with the least amount of disruption.

situation 2 – Steph

Steph is also a trainee in the Accounts Department. She is currently studying for her AAT Level 3 having successfully completed the AAT Level 2 Diploma in Accounting and Business. She has just found out that she has failed the last exam to complete the qualification for the second time.

Mo asks:

> *'Are you going to carry on with your studying or does this mean you will give up?'*

Steph replies:

> *'No way! If at first you don't succeed try, try again! I've already booked a revision course at the end of the month and I'm going to sit the exam again as soon as my tutor thinks I'm ready. I'm determined to achieve this qualification however long it takes.'*

Steph's personal skills – initiative, commitment and perseverance

Steph has suffered a setback having not passed her exam. However, she is showing **initiative** by booking herself on a revision course, **commitment** by being determined to complete her qualification and **perseverance** by keeping going despite having been unsuccessful in two attempts at this final exam.

situation 3 – Riley

Riley, the Accounts Supervisor, overhears the conversation between Mo and Steph. Rather than interrupt she decides to send the following email to Steph:

To:	steph@gradyssupplies.com
From:	riley@gradyssupplies.com
Date:	Wednesday, 28 May 20XX, 10.43
Subject:	Exams

Hi Steph,

I'm really sorry that you failed your last exam again; I know how hard you worked for it. It's a few years since I finished my AAT but if you thought it would be helpful I would be very happy to do some revision with you during a few lunch breaks. After all we're all part of a team.

Best wishes

Riley

Riley's personal skills – commitment

By 'going the extra mile' and offering to give up her time to help Steph with her revision Riley is showing **commitment** to the team that she works with.

EMBRACING CHANGE

what does 'embracing change' mean?

'**Embracing change**' means:

'dealing with and making the most of change and seeing change as a challenge rather than a threat'

The phrase 'embracing change' may seem a bit abstract and vague, but it does relate to a very important personal skill – that of being able to deal with situations that involve changes in the workplace.

Examples of these changes include:

- a change in the skills required for a particular job, for example, the **computerisation of an accounting system** – this will mean that previously learnt practical skills such as manual double-entry and invoicing will not be needed so much and computer-based skills will be required instead
- extra training will be needed so that **new skills and knowledge** can be learnt
- **restructuring of a business** – which can result from relocation or introduction of new management – may change **the nature of tasks**, ie what you have to do on a day-to-day basis, and also **where** you have to work
- **patterns of working** may change and the traditional 9.00 to 5.00 working day may disappear, for example if '**flexitime**' is introduced: this is a system which allows flexible working hours at the beginning or end of each day, provided an agreed period of each day (eg 5 hours) is spent at the place of work

an employee's reaction to change

The reaction of an employee to any of these workplace changes can range from

- a **negative approach**: 'I prefer to do what I am used to and can't be doing with all this change' to
- a **positive attitude**: 'I can see advantages in the new system – I can learn new skills and the hours of work will allow me more time with my family

It is the positive reaction to change which will enable the employee to 'embrace change' by developing new skills, changing priorities, and hopefully enjoying a better life/work balance.

Case Study

MYERS TYRES – EMBRACING CHANGE

situation

John Myers the owner and Managing Director of a successful tyre manufacturer, Myers Tyres, has recently retired and his daughter Hayley has taken over. She has sent the following email to all staff.

To: all staff
From: hayley@myerstyres.com
Date: Friday, 14th February 20XX, 4.04pm
Subject: Flexitime

Dear all,

Please find attached details of the new flexitime working scheme for all employees at Myers Tyres. All members of staff will continue to work 35 hours per week and must be on site between 10am and 2pm each day. However the remaining hours can be worked anytime within the business opening hours of 8am to 6pm. A computerised timesheet system will be implemented to record hours worked under the new system.

I am holding a brief Question and Answer Session on Monday morning at 10am where you can raise any queries that you have.

I hope you all have a pleasant weekend.

Best wishes

Hayley

Monday morning arrives and a large number of the workforce turn up for the meeting with Hayley. The following questions and comments are raised at the meeting:

Stan, a fifty-year-old machine operator:

> *'I've been working here for 30 years. I get in at 8.30am and I leave at 4.30pm with an hour for lunch. Are you telling me I'm going to have to come in at 10am and stay until 6pm? I'll see even less of my grandchildren if that happens!'*

Virat, a customer services assistant:

> *'I read the documents on flexitime working and I think it's a great idea even though I realise there will be times when I'm the only person in the department. If I work 8am until 4.30pm Monday to Thursday I can work 9am until 2pm on a Friday. That means on four days I'll miss the rush hour on the way into work and on Fridays I can set off at lunchtime to visit my girlfriend in Scotland.'*

Xavier, the accounts department manager:

'I'm concerned that all my staff will want to do what Virat plans to do and I'll end up being the only one in the office on a Friday afternoon. If it's acceptable I propose that in my department we let each other know in advance if we plan to leave early because of flexitime and we share out Friday afternoons off fairly if it proves to be popular – as I suspect it will.'

How do these three employees deal with the proposed changes at Myers Tyres?

In other words, to what extent do they 'embrace change'?

Stan, a fifty-year-old machine operator:

Stan has had the same routine for 30 years. His reaction is to be expected. He has misunderstood the proposal. If he had looked at it more carefully he would realise that he could 'flex' his working day and see more of his family rather than less.

Stan is not currently embracing the change.

Virat, a customer services assistant:

Virat has taken time to read through the proposal. He has identified that on occasions he may be the only person in the office and that this may put more pressure on him. However he has also seen the opportunities that it gives him and is planning how the system will work for him.

Virat is definitely embracing the change.

Xavier, the accounts department manager:

Xavier is showing some initial concerns about the proposed new system and seems quick to identify the negatives in the system. However, he has suggested a workable solution in his department and dealt with the challenge rather than seeing the proposed change as a threat.

Xavier has seen problems but has found a solution that will allow him to embrace the change.

Chapter Summary

- Personal skills are very different from the communication skills covered in previous chapters, eg writing emails and documenting meetings.
- Personal skills are more general and relate to an employee's personality and ability to deal with people and situations in the workplace.
- Personal skills are also transferable, in other words they can be used in everyday family life.
- Personal skills include:
  - managing time
  - initiative
  - commitment
  - perseverance
  - embracing change

  These are all explained in more detail in the Key Terms below.

Key Terms

personal skills — skills which can be used and developed not only in the workplace but also in everyday life

transferable skills — skills such as personal skills which can be used in a variety of different situations

managing time — planning ahead and dealing with unexpected events, being punctual, being able to prioritise and distinguish between urgent and important tasks

initiative — assessing and working out what needs to be done and then completing the task; it also involves helping others, providing ideas and being decisive

commitment — 'doing what it takes' by fully completing all tasks given, supporting colleagues and the employer

perseverance — 'sticking at it' and 'keeping going whatever happens' when at work or taking exams

embracing change — dealing with and making the most of change in the workplace, seeing change as a challenge rather than a threat, showing a positive attitude

Activities

6.1 Decide which of the following factors you should bear in mind when you are prioritising your work.

Select one option.

		✔
(a)	How much you enjoy doing the tasks	
(b)	The urgency and importance of the tasks	
(c)	Your own strengths and weaknesses in doing the tasks	
(d)	How scary and strict the manager is who asks you to do the tasks	

6.2 Neil's manager is very pleased with the report that he volunteered to produce at the last team meeting. The report shows any increase in spending by customers who had received the company's monthly marketing email for the first time.

Neil has also included details of all the customers that have unsubscribed (ie have asked not to receive any further emails) in relation to the amount they had spent in the previous month. Neil thought this report might be useful for marketing purposes even though it meant that he had to work late to complete it by the deadline the manager had set.

Indicate which two of the following options shows Neil using his initiative.

		✔
(a)	Volunteering to produce the report	
(b)	Hitting the deadline he had been set	
(c)	Not charging any overtime for producing the report	
(d)	Including the additional information about customers who unsubscribed	

6.3 It is 4.30pm and your manager has just realised that he needs an analysis of the business's trade receivables (money owed by customers) for a very important meeting at 10am tomorrow morning.

Your supervisor who would normally do this is away on holiday. Decide which one of the following actions on your part would show commitment.

		✔
(a)	Telephone your supervisor and tell him he needs to come in first thing in the morning and produce the report	
(b)	Volunteer to stay late yourself and produce the report	
(c)	Sympathise with your manager when he says he will have to do it	
(d)	Suggest that the manager postpones the meeting	

6.4 Sharon is the Accounts Assistant in a firm of solicitors. She has been asked by the Accounts Supervisor to transfer all the year-end amounts owed by the firm's clients from the old computerised accounting system to a new one. Sharon has transferred all 143 client balances, but the total of all the account balances on the new system does not agree with the total on the old one.

Decide which one of the following demonstrates perseverance shown by Sharon in solving the problem.

	✔
(a) She tells the supervisor that it's all done and goes home hoping no one will notice	
(b) She tells the supervisor that she has not been able to make the transfer successfully and someone else will have to do it	
(c) Having tried to find the difference she re-inputs the balances, checking each one thoroughly before moving onto the next	
(d) She tells the supervisor that she has done the transfer but there is a difference which someone will need to investigate	

6.5 Joybell Cleaning is a successful domestic and commercial cleaning business. It was set up six years ago by two sisters, Joyce and Annabel, and has grown rapidly since then. The business has always used manual timesheets for the cleaners to record their hours but is about to introduce an electronic system that uses a satellite navigate system (GPS) to track where each cleaner is at any time. This automatically calculates how many hours are worked for each client. There has been mixed reaction to the new system.

For each of the following statements made by members of staff decide whether they are 'embracing change' or 'not embracing change'. Tick one of the two columns for each option.

	Embracing change ✔	**Not embracing change** ✔
(a) 'That's good as I won't have to come back to the office after work on a Friday to get my time sheet authorised'		
(b) 'Is this just another way of reducing how much we get paid?'		
(c) 'It would be a really good idea if the system could show us a summary of the work we've done so we can check that we agree with it'		
(d) 'Sounds like Big Brother will be watching us!'		
(e) 'This will mean that we have proof of how many hours we've been at a job if they query the bill'		
(f) 'It might take a bit of getting used to but at least I don't have to rely on my memory when I'm completing my timesheet at the end of the week'		

7 Evaluating skills

this chapter covers...

Communication skills and personal skills are essential in business and it is important that employees should evaluate and develop their skills. This chapter covers the following topics:

- *the need for employees to assess their communication and personal skills*
- *employees can measure their skills in a particular job against a job description and a person specification*
- *the skills needed for working in business are set out in a 'person specification'*
- *a 'person specification' is different from a 'job description' which sets out 'what you have to do' when you take on a job*
- *input from colleagues and management can help employees set future goals for skills they need to achieve so that they can be effective and efficient in the workplace*
- *goals (objectives) can be short-term (up to one year) and long-term (up to five years)*
- *objectives should be SMART, ie Specific, Measurable, Achievable, Realistic, Time bound*
- *employees should be given feedback from colleagues and managers so that they can review how they have developed their skills and then plan ahead to achieve further goals*

WHAT ARE THE SKILLS?

In this book so far we have described in detail the different types of skills that are needed for working in business. These can be divided into two types:

- **communication skills**

  These are specific skills that are needed for effective communication within a business and also for communicating with other organisations and with customers. They involve communicating using:

  - **emails and letters**: writing them using appropriate business language and knowing how to set them out and what to include
  - **telephones**: using landlines and mobiles to express yourself clearly and in line with the policies and procedures of the business
  - **meetings**: knowing how to contribute to a meeting and the documentation (agenda, minutes) that is used to set out what is to be covered and what is discussed at the meeting

- **personal skills**

  These are skills that are needed within a business but are also useful in everyday life outside the workplace. They include managing time, using initiative, showing commitment, being able to persevere (keep going) and ready to deal with changes when they occur.

  These skills are set out in the following diagram:

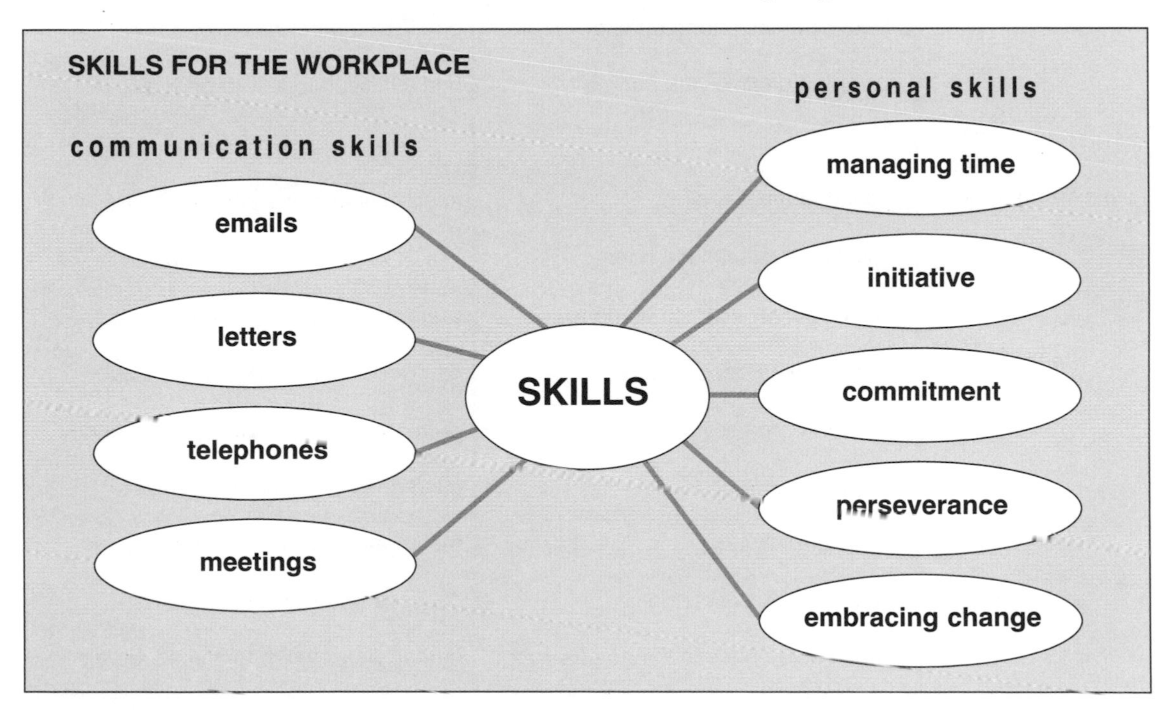

THE IMPORTANCE OF ASSESSING SKILLS

applying for a job – assessing your skills

When applying for a job it is important that you think about what your skills are and whether you are suitable for that job. For example, if you are inexperienced in dealing with the public and prefer working on your own you may not be best suited to dealing with customer complaints in a Customer Services role. If you are confident and like dealing with people and problem solving you could be ideal for the job.

strengths and weaknesses

When you are thinking about the sort of job to apply for, it is a good idea to carry out a **skills analysis** and list your strong points and your weak areas, in other words your **strengths** and **weaknesses**. Obviously it is your skills that you will want to highlight when applying for a job.

Here are some examples of strengths and weaknesses relating to the communication skills and personal skills covered earlier in this book:

	STRENGTHS	WEAKNESSES
communication skills	good standard of written English	problems with written English
	excellent telephone manner	can lose temper easily on phone
	good at dealing with people	find it difficult to talk to people
personal skills	good at timekeeping	keep oversleeping and being late
	flexible over working hours	like to keep to a set timetable
	flexible over tasks to be done	prefer to do the same tasks
	can work under pressure	can get stressed and 'lose it' easily
	good at organising people	prefer to be given tasks by someone
	enjoy solving problems	mind goes blank under pressure
	enjoy teamwork	feel threatened by other people
	have a positive outlook	cautious and wary of problems
	don't give up when things go wrong	tend to panic when things go wrong

job descriptions and person specifications

It is useful when applying for a job to find out if there is a job description and/or person specification available for the job advertised. These sound like the same thing but in fact they are quite different.

It is important to be aware of the difference:

A '**job description**' sets out the job title, the tasks that have to be done and the responsibilities of the job. In other words it describes 'what you will have to do' to carry out the job and fit into the structure of the business.

A '**person specification**' on the other hand, lists the attributes that a person needs for carrying out the job, ie the skills, experience and qualifications. In other words it is 'what the employer is looking for and wants you to bring to the job'.

When you have identified and written down your strengths and weaknesses (see the previous page) you can then:

- make sure that you are capable of carrying out all the tasks listed in the **job description** – for example if you need to create spreadsheets or drive a car and have no experience of spreadsheets or have no driving licence, you will need to apply somewhere else for a job
- map your skills (your 'strengths'), your experience and qualifications against the details in the **person specification**

what if there is no job description or person specification?

It may be that the employer does not have a job description or person specification drawn up. The job may be as a temp serving in a fast food restaurant or filling shelves in a supermarket. What do you do then?

If this is the case you should identify all the **relevant strengths** in your skills assessment (see previous page) which match up with the job and make sure that you make the prospective employer aware of them, either on an application form or at an interview.

For example, if you are applying for a job in a fast food outlet, the ability to be good at dealing with people and being prepared to work flexible hours will be big advantages in your favour from the employer's point of view.

You should also look at your **weaknesses** and make sure that none of them will make the job very difficult or impossible for you. If, for example, you find it difficult working under pressure, working in a fast food environment may not be a good idea.

There are examples on the next page of a basic job description and person specification for the same accounting job. You should note the differences.

JOB DESCRIPTION

Job Title	Senior Accounts Assistant
Job details	A Senior Accounts Assistant to work in a busy Accounts Department at Henwickford Mouldings Limited in their St Johns office. He or she will assist managers and supervise junior accounting staff in a range of accounting and finance functions.
Position	**Reports to:** Accounts Manager **Responsible for:** Six Accounts Assistants
Main duties	Sales Ledger and Credit Control Purchase Ledger Payroll Banking transactions Petty cash
Previous experience	The candidate should ideally have experience in a commercial Accounts Department at Assistant level. He or she should be competent in dealing with sales and purchases documentation, Sage computer accounting systems, cash handling, banking and petty cash procedures.

PERSON SPECIFICATION

Experience required	Henwickford Mouldings Limited is looking for a candidate who has had previous employment as an Accounts Assistant in a manufacturing business covering the areas of documentation, bookkeeping, Sage computer accounting and cash and banking procedures.
Skills required	The candidate should be: – accurate and analytical – numerate – familiar with Sage 50 – a good communicator – a team player – able to work under pressure
Qualifications	The candidate should have GCSEs grades A*-C in English and Maths, and should ideally be currently studying for an accounting qualification offered by Awarding Bodies such as the Association of Accounting Technicians, the Institute of Certified Bookkeepers and City & Guilds.

RAJ – ANALYSING SKILLS FOR EMPLOYMENT

situation

Raj has recently left school and enrolled on an AAT course at his local college. He has previously done some work experience at a local charity shop and is now looking for a part-time job that fits in with his college work. He has found three jobs in the local newspaper that he thinks might be suitable. These are:

1. Working variable hours as a waiter in a popular local pizza restaurant
2. Working in a large team at a local call centre for a national courier service three evenings a week
3. Working on the checkout at a local supermarket two late evenings and Sunday afternoon

Raj has gathered together the following information so that he can analyse and assess his skills to help him decide which job to go for.

report from Raj's work experience placement

The manager of the charity shop wrote in his report to the school:

> *'Raj is a very polite young man who is not afraid of hard work. He was good at dealing with customers although he got very nervous when he had to make or receive phone calls. Raj was always punctual and arrived at 9am every morning. He was not keen to work beyond 5pm when the shop closed.'*

report from Raj's school

Raj's form teacher at school wrote in his final report:

> *'Raj is a hard worker who prefers to work on his own. He does not enjoy working under pressure but provided he is given clear instructions he will work well independently and get the work done without complaining.'*

From this information Raj analyses his skills into strengths and weaknesses to help him decide which of the three jobs would be most suitable for him.

solution

Raj's strengths

- Good at dealing with customers face-to-face
- Good at timekeeping
- Works well independently
- Gets the job done

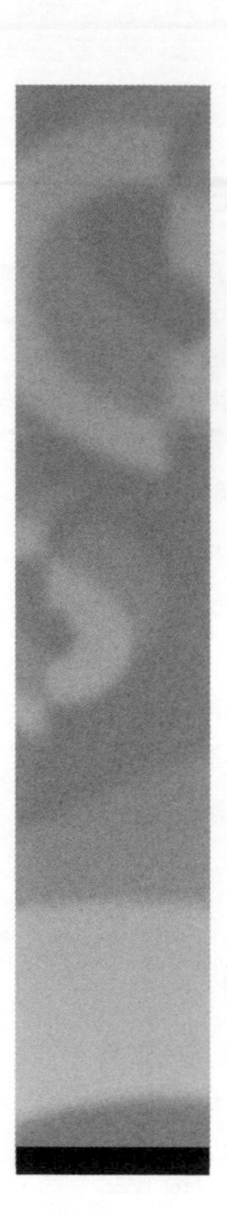

Raj's weaknesses

- Not good at speaking on the telephone
- Likes to keep to a set timetable
- Prefers not to work in a team
- Does not like working under pressure

Raj's conclusions

Assessing his skills in this way – identifying his strengths and weaknesses – leads Raj to think that the job at the local pizza restaurant may not suit him. Despite being good at dealing with customers face-to-face he likes to keep to a set timetable and does not like working under pressure.

The job in the call centre would also not be suitable as he is not good at speaking on the telephone and prefers not to work in a team.

Raj decides that the best part-time job for him to apply for would be working in the supermarket. His reasoning is:

- he is good at dealing with customers face-to-face
- his timekeeping is good so he won't be late
- he can work independently which he will have to do at the checkout
- once he knows what is required of him he gets the job done
- most supermarkets have fixed times for shifts so the fact that he likes to keep to a set timetable will not be a problem

SETTING GOALS

the importance of skills analysis

As a student you will hopefully be in a position where you have had experience of a work environment. It may be that you:

- already have a temporary full-time job to earn money (holiday job)
- already have a regular part-time job to earn money (weekend or evening work)
- have done work experience or work shadowing
- have heard from other students how they have got on when at work

In this case you will be in a position to:

- know what skills are required in the workplace
- be familiar with some of the tasks carried out in the workplace

This will set you up for carrying out a **skills analysis** which is described earlier in this chapter – setting out what you are good at (your **strengths**) and what you are not good at (your **weaknesses**).

You can then see how well your '**skills set**' (all the things you are good at) fits in with the job that you are doing or hoping to apply for.

setting skills goals in a job

Skills analysis can also be used once you are in a job to set 'goals' – targets for improvement in both **communication skills** and **personal skills**.

These are normally agreed with your employer when you have your yearly **job appraisal**. This will involve you sitting down with a manager and discussing:

- your own assessment of how you think you are getting on
- your employer's assessment of how they think you are getting on at work
- your progress with qualifications you may be taking
- your strengths and weaknesses

When you have discussed these points with your manager, you can then set goals for the future. Achieving your goals can take time, they can be:

- **short-term** – up to **one year**: eg improving your communication and personal skills by attending an external two day Customer Services course
- **long-term** – up to **five years**: eg taking an AAT qualification by attending evening classes at a local College for three or four years

skills development – effectiveness and efficiency

Skills development benefits not only the employee but also the employer. Skilled employees are employees that become both **effective** and **efficient**. These terms sound very similar but are actually different.

'**Effective**' means producing the result that you have planned for. In business, a sales team that achieves its sales targets will be 'effective' and contribute to the profitability of the business.

'**Efficient**' means getting the job done with the minimum waste of effort and resources. This is, of course, an important objective in any organisation.

Employees who develop their skills and become both effective and efficient become very valuable to their employer.

SMART goals

When setting short-term and long-term goals you should always aim for **SMART** objectives. **SMART** stands for:

Specific
Measurable
Achievable
Realistic
Time bound

The meaning of these terms is as follows:

- **Specific** – each goal or target set should be clearly explained so that the employee knows what is expected and the manager can monitor and assess how successful the employee is in achieving the goal.
- **Measurable** – the employee and the manager should be able to tell how successfully the goal is being achieved. For example, if the employee is taking an AAT qualification, the employee will need to show that he or she has passed the assessments.
- **Achievable** – the goal must be something which the employee can actually do. The employer can help here, for example by paying for an external training course.
- **Realistic** – this is similar to 'achievable' and asks whether the employee is happy to work to achieve the goal. Does the employee have the necessary commitment?
- **Time bound** – a timescale must be set for the goal. Can it be achieved within the target time? Remember that goals can be short-term (within one year) but also long-term (within five years). Qualifications, for example, can take several years to complete.

TOMAS – ACHIEVING 'SMART' OBJECTIVES

situation

Tomas is an Accounts Assistant at Yellowbrick Travel, a company that arranges 'dream holidays' such as honeymoons.

It is 1 February and Tomas has just had his annual job appraisal with his manager. After a long discussion they have identified two goals for Tomas.

A summary of the discussion follows on the next page.

goal 1 – spreadsheet skills

Tomas has excellent spreadsheet skills, which he is keen to use in the workplace. He has been asked to set up a spreadsheet that analyses the sales of the business for the last two years:

- by geographical destination
- on a month-by-month basis
- ensuring the monthly destination figures agree to the total monthly sales

Tomas estimates that taking into account the time he has free after doing his routine work the spreadsheet will take him two to three months to complete. His manager has set the completion date as 30 April, ie three months ahead.

goal 2 – an AAT qualification

Tomas is keen to gain a recognised accounting qualification and he and his manager have agreed that he should enrol on an AAT course at the local college. Tomas will start at Level 2 in the first year and then do Levels 3 and 4 in the following two years. His manager has agreed that if Tomas attends the college two evenings a week for three years then Yellowbrick Travel will pay the course fees.

TASK

Explain to Tomas whether each of these two goals is short-term or long-term and to what extent the objectives they involve are 'SMART'.

solution – short-term or long-term goals?

Goal 1 is a short-term objective as the spreadsheet is required within three months – which is less than one year.

Goal 2 is a long-term objective as the plan is that it will take Tomas three years to complete his AAT qualification.

solution – how 'SMART' are the objectives?

SMART objectives are those that are Specific, Measurable, Achievable, Realistic and Time bound.

goal 1 – spreadsheet skills

Specific	The task is clearly explained so Tomas knows how he has to set up the required sales spreadsheet.
Measurable	The success of the spreadsheet can be measured by how useful it is to the manager and whether the overall totals agree with the monthly sales figures.
Achievable	Tomas has excellent spreadsheet skills so he should be able to achieve the goal of producing the sales spreadsheet.

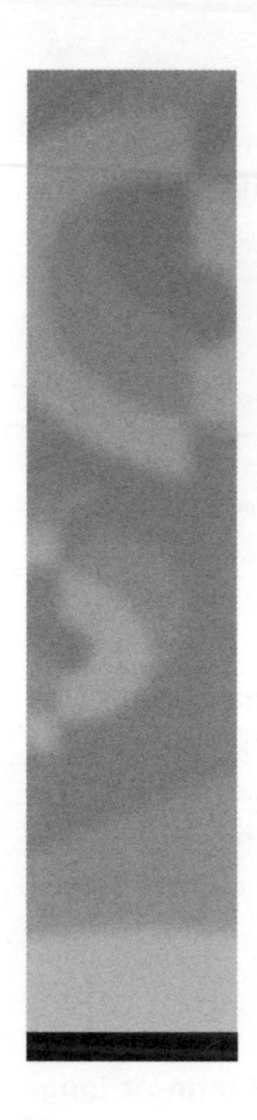

Realistic	Tomas is keen to use his spreadsheet skills in the workplace.
Time bound	The manager has set the timescale for producing the spreadsheet as three months. Tomas believes that it will take him two to three months to complete, which indicates that the time target can be achieved.

goal 2 – an AAT qualification

Specific	The objective is for Tomas to complete his AAT qualification by passing his exams.
Measurable	Tomas's success can be measured as he passes each level of the AAT exams.
Achievable	Tomas's manager believes that Tomas can achieve the AAT qualification or he would not have suggested that he takes it. The business has agreed to pay for the course for three years.
Realistic	Tomas is keen to gain a recognised accounting qualification, which indicates that he has the necessary commitment to study for it.
Time bound	The timescale given by the manager for completing the three levels of the AAT qualification is three years.

FEEDBACK AND REVIEW

forms of feedback

When you have completed a skills analysis and set goals to improve your communication and personal skills it is important to monitor your progress on a regular basis. One way of doing this is to receive **feedback** from others.

Feedback can come from a number of sources. If you are at work it could be a manager, supervisor or a colleague; if you are still studying it is likely to be your tutor/teacher. Feedback can be:

- **formal** – eg an annual appraisal in a work situation or a tutor/teacher interview at college or school
- **informal** – in a work situation it could be comments from colleagues or a supervisor/manager; at college or school it could be praise or criticism from the tutor/teacher and even from fellow students

the need to review

Remember that goals may be short-term (within one year) or long-term (within five years). After these periods the goals should be reviewed. Feedback is brought into the discussion when you **review** your progress and skills development and set a **new skills analysis** in motion. The process of skills analysis and the creation of new goals then start all over again.

This process is illustrated in the diagram below – you should read it from left to right, following the time line shown at the bottom.

Then read the Case Study which follows – this explains how Tomas can review his goals and set new ones.

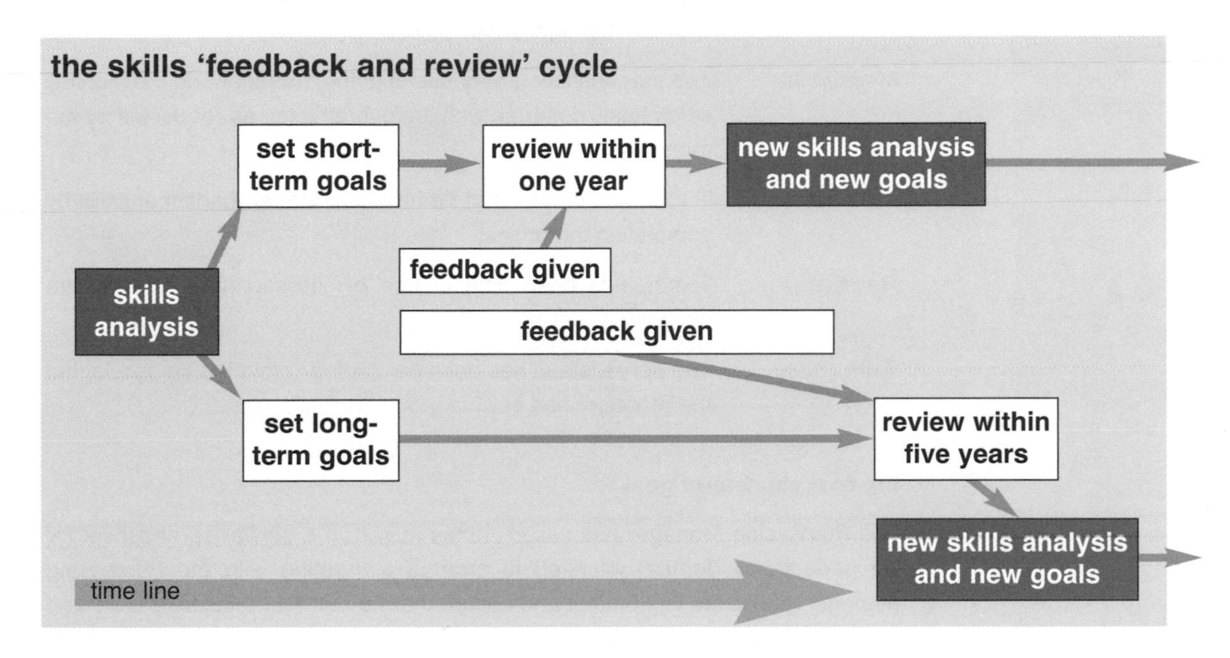

Case Study

TOMAS – REVIEWING 'SMART' OBJECTIVES

situation 1 – Tomas three months later

We now return to Tomas from the previous Case Study which starts on page 106.

It is 5 May and Tomas is having a meeting with his manager to assess whether he has successfully achieved the short-term goal set at his annual appraisal.

The manager says to Tomas:

'It was good to receive the first monthly sales spreadsheet on 16 April; it's always helpful to get something ahead of schedule. I have had a good look at it and I'm very impressed with the way in which it works – the automatic function which checks that the monthly sales totals agree is a very professional touch. If you can ensure that you keep this up-to-date I'm sure all the managers in the department will find it very useful. The Purchasing Manager has already asked whether you could set up something similar for his department.'

TASK 1

Explain whether Tomas has achieved the 'SMART' goal he was set and what his next short-term goal might be.

The feedback on Tomas's spreadsheet from his manager is very positive. The targets set by the 'SMART' objectives have all been met:

Specific Tomas has produced a very well-designed spreadsheet in line with the manager's instructions.

Measurable The spreadsheet is very useful to the manager and the monthly sales totals do agree with the overall total, as requested by the manager.

Achievable Tomas has proved that he has excellent spreadsheet skills by completing the project.

Realistic Tomas has been able to use his spreadsheet skills in the workplace.

Time bound The spreadsheet has been completed within the timescale that the manager had set.

the next short-term goal

The Purchasing Manager has asked Tomas to set up a similar spreadsheet for his department. Tomas will need to arrange a meeting with the Purchasing Manager to discuss this project and ensure that he has the necessary skills and that the new goal is also 'SMART'.

situation 2 – Tomas three years later

Time has moved on three years and Tomas is now an Accounts Supervisor at Yellowbrick Travel and reports to a different manager. He is currently having his annual job appraisal. This is what happened at the appraisal:

Tomas's new manager congratulates him on completing his AAT Level 4 qualification – a goal that was initially set at his annual job appraisal three years earlier. He is particularly pleased that Tomas has managed to complete the three levels within the three year timescale set at the earlier appraisal meeting.

Tomas is keen to continue with his accounting studies and wants to enrol on an ACCA course, but he cannot afford to pay for it himself. The nearest college offering this course is one hour on the train from Yellowbrick Travel's office and the course runs from 5.30pm on a Wednesday and Thursday evening. Tomas does not normally finish work until 5pm.

Tomas has achieved his long-term goal of an AAT qualification within the three year timescale.

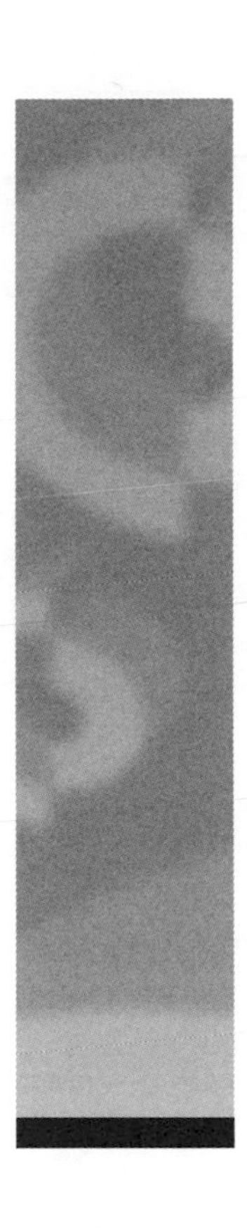

TASK 2

Explain how Tomas and his manager can ensure that his new long-term goal of completing an ACCA qualification can be 'SMART':

Tomas and his manager discuss plans for enabling Tomas to study the most appropriate ACCA course. These are the 'SMART' objectives they established:

Specific	Tomas wants to study for ACCA. As there are two levels of ACCA he and his manager will need to decide which level he will study for and set his objective to achieve this level.
Measurable	Tomas's success can be measured as he passes each exam.
Achievable	Tomas and his manager need to discuss whether Yellowbrick Travel will pay for the ACCA course and also whether it will be possible for Tomas to leave work sufficiently early to get to the course on time. Only then will the goal be achievable.
Realistic	Tomas has achieved success in his AAT studies and is keen to continue but the ACCA course will mean him giving up two evenings and spending a lot of time travelling.
Time bound	Tomas and his manager will need to discuss a sensible timescale for him to achieve his goal of completing the ACCA qualification.

Chapter Summary

- Well developed skills – including communication skills and personal skills – are needed in business and will help you get a job.
- It is useful to draw up a list of your skills and then assess them when deciding whether a particular job is suitable for you.
- A skills assessment involves identifying your strengths and weaknesses in those skills.
- If you are applying for a job it is helpful to obtain a job description to see what the job involves and also a person specification to see what skills are required.
- If you are in employment you should set short-term and long-term goals for skills development. These skills should ideally be SMART (see Key Terms).
- Employees developing good skills benefit the employer by becoming both effective and efficient.
- Employees should review their progress in skills development at regular intervals to see if they have achieved their goals.
- It is important to take notice of feedback from colleagues and the employer when assessing skills development.
- An important part of the skills review process is to set new goals for further review in the future.

Key Terms

communication skills	skills needed to communicate, either in writing or by word of mouth
personal skills	skills which can be used and developed not only in the workplace but also in everyday life
job description	a document which sets out the job title, the tasks and the responsibilities of a job
person specification	a document which sets out what is needed from the employee to do the job, ie the skills, experience and qualifications
skills analysis	a critical look at an employee's skills, weighing up strengths and weaknesses
job appraisal	a yearly interview with a manager or supervisor assessing an employee's progress with work tasks, skills development and progress with qualifications
short-term goals	targets set for achievement in areas such as skills development within one year
long-term goals	targets set for achievement in areas such as skills development within five years
SMART goals	Goals (objectives) set for an employee which are: **Specific** – a goal clearly and precisely explained **Measurable** – it should be possible to measure the success of the goal **Achievable** – a goal which must be something the employee can actually do **Realistic** – a goal to which the employee will be committed and happy to achieve **Time bound** – a timescale and time limit must be set for the completion of the goal

Activities

7.1 Complete the following statement about evaluating skills by selecting the appropriate words from the selection in bold below (not all the words will be needed).

'When thinking about what job to apply for you should first carry out a .... to identify your .... and ....'

job appraisal **job description** **person specification**

weaknesses **skills analysis** **strengths**

7.2 Complete the sentences below by selecting the correct word from these two options in bold:

job description **person specification**

'A .... sets out the job title, the tasks that have to be done and the responsibilities of the job.'

'A .... lists the skills, experience and qualifications that an individual needs for carrying out the job.'

7.3 Complete the following statement by inserting the appropriate number of years in each space.

'Goals that are set at a job appraisal can be short-term goals or long-term goals. Short-term goals are those that you plan to achieve in up to .... year(s) and long-term goals are those that you plan to achieve in up to .... year(s).'

7.4 A goal can be described as 'SMART'. These five letters stand for five types of objective.

Complete the table below by writing in the appropriate words to describe these objectives.

S	
M	
A	
R	
T	

7.5 Val is an Accounts Assistant. During a job appraisal she has been given the objective of setting up full details of the business's 400 customers on the new company database. Val or her manager made the following statements during the appraisal meeting.

For each statement decide which SMART objective it fulfils. Write this SMART objective underneath the appropriate statement. Use each objective only once.

Manager:	'The project must be completed by the end of September.'
SMART objective	....
Manager:	'You can allocate one day per week to complete this project.'
SMART objective	....
Val:	'I'm really going to work hard to get this database up and running.'
SMART objective	....
Manager:	'I have set up a standard template for each customer for you to use. All 400 customers need to be added to the database.'
SMART objective	....
Val:	'Once I have completed the database I will get my supervisor, Jill, to test it to make sure it meets the department's needs.'
SMART objective	....

7.6 Skills development produces skilled employees that are both efficient and effective. This benefits both the employee and employer.

Decide whether the two definitions below refer to being either efficient or effective by ticking the appropriate column.

	Efficient ✔	Effective ✔
Producing the result that you have planned for.		
Getting the job done with the minimum waste of effort and resources.		

7.7 Read the following statements about feedback and decide whether the feedback is formal or informal. Tick the appropriate column.

	Formal ✔	Informal ✔
A work colleague says the spreadsheet you have produced is very useful.		
At your annual job appraisal your manager says that he is very pleased with the new filing system you have organised and set up.		
Your tutor tells you in class that your class attendance is unacceptable and that you need to improve this in order to pass your course.		
Your classmate tells you that you have got the double-entry question you are doing in class wrong.		

8 Problem solving and team working

this chapter covers...

Effective communication skills and personal skills are needed by an employee in a business workplace not only to sort out potential areas of dissatisfaction and conflict but also to become an effective team member. This chapter covers the following topics:

- *the importance of developing communication skills in order to deal with potential problems in the workplace such as:*
  - *employees not having enough information or having the wrong information*
  - *people who have problems or complaints*
- *the importance of developing personal skills in order to become an effective employee – for example, managing time, showing initiative, having commitment and being able to keep going and deal with difficulties and problems that occur*
- *the reasons why teams are needed in the workplace – eg for planning, routine administration, sorting out a particular problem such as a staffing shortage*
- *the communication and personal skills that are needed in order to become an effective member of a team in the workplace*
- *developing specific skills in order to take up a specific team role – eg leading a meeting, resolving a dispute*
- *the need for employees to be able to work out a strategy for achieving a positive result from teamwork – eg by negotiation between team members and setting clear goals for what needs to be done*
- *the need for employees to develop social skills, ie to be courteous (polite) and helpful and to show respect to colleagues*

THE NEED FOR COMMUNICATION SKILLS

what are business communication skills?

Earlier in this book we have seen that a range of communication skills should be developed by employees so that they become competent in dealing with:

- emails and letters
- telephones
- meetings

All these ways of communicating involve passing on information. In a workplace, or when dealing with people outside the business, it is very important that:

- the information is passed on to the **right person**, or people
- the **correct** information is passed on
- **all** the information is passed on
- the information is passed on **clearly**
- the information is passed on **within the right timescale** – this could be immediately or sometime tomorrow, or next week

what can go wrong and cause problems?

When communication is not made to the right person (or people) on time, or is incomplete, incorrect or unclear, there may be misunderstandings and problems. The following examples will give you an idea of what can go wrong.

example of information sent to the wrong person

You are an Accounts Assistant and have been asked by your manager to send an up-to-date sales spreadsheet to Alex Johnson, a Sales Manager, who is attending a senior management meeting. Unfortunately you send it to Alec Johnston who works in Marketing.

Result: the wrong person gets the spreadsheet and the Sales Manager is unable to report the sales results at the meeting.

example of incorrect information given

You are asked to arrange for a taxi to pick up an important visitor to your company. You phone and tell the taxi company to pick up from 'Main Street Station' when in fact you were told it was 'Parkway Station'.

Result: the visitor is left waiting at Parkway Station and has to get his own taxi to your premises. This gives him a poor impression of your company.

example of incomplete information given

You are an Accounts Assistant and have been asked by your Line Manager to print out from the computer a list of customers who have not paid their invoices on time, as he wants to chase up the debts. Unfortunately, as you are in a hurry you accidentally leave the last sheet printed out in the printer tray.

Result: the Line Manager does not chase up all the overdue debts as a number of customers who have not paid up on time are missing from his list. This means that the company is still owed that money.

example of unclear information given

You are a Sales Assistant and take an order over the telephone. You write down the details on an order form but your writing is difficult to read. As a result the person processing the order gets the product details wrong.

Result: the customer is sent the wrong goods and is not pleased; she complains and returns the incorrect goods for a refund.

example of information given where the timing is wrong

You are an Accounts Assistant and one of your regular tasks is to provide the sales figures at the end of each month to the Marketing Department; these figures are needed for the monthly management meetings. You are going on holiday in the first week of June and in your rush to finish everything in the last week of May, you forget to pass on the figures.

Result: the Marketing Department does not get the figures on time and the management meeting has to be postponed until they can be provided by somebody else in the Accounts Department.

conclusion

You will see from all these examples that there has been a breakdown in communication resulting in misunderstandings and problems.

If the person making the communication in the first place had exercised proper communication skills – ie if the communication had been complete, accurate, clear, to the right person and on time, the misunderstandings and problems could have been avoided.

The problems discussed above have resulted from poor **communication skills**. On the next couple of pages we look at how problems and misunderstandings can be put right by using the **personal skills** described in Chapter 6.

SOLVING PROBLEMS USING PERSONAL SKILLS

communication skills and personal skills

Good **communication skills** will help to make the running of a business more efficient and problem free. But there are situations that arise which need more than just the ability to communicate well. We will now take a look at the way that **personal skills** can be used to help solve problems.

As we saw in Chapter 6, personal skills are more 'general' than communication skills and relate to:

- your personality
- your ability to deal with people, situations and problems

Personal skills can be used not only in business but also as **transferable skills** in your everyday relationships with friends and family.

To recap what was stated in Chapter 6, personal skills include:

- **managing time**, which involves planning ahead and dealing with unexpected events
- **initiative**, which means 'seeing what needs to be done and then getting on and doing it'
- **commitment**, which means 'doing what it takes' and showing loyalty to people and organisations
- **perseverance**, a rather old-fashioned word which means 'sticking at it' or 'keeping going whatever happens'
- **embracing change**, which means 'dealing with and making the most of change', in other words seeing change as a challenge rather than a threat

personal skills in your assessment

As part of your assessment you may be required to:

- identify a personal skill needed in the workplace which can be used to solve a specific problem
- suggest a solution to that problem using the personal skill that you have identified

The diagram on the next page and the Case Study that follows give examples of how this 'identification of a personal skill' process works in practice.

personal skills	situations they can help with
managing time	If you cannot manage your time, you will get yourself in a muddle and also let other people down by not meeting deadlines. If you have more tasks to do than you have time available for them, you can manage your time by: – prioritising your tasks by writing a 'to do' list – asking someone else to help you – telling your manager that you may need help
showing initiative	This means assessing what needs to be done and then making it happen. Initiative is an essential part of being a good leader or manager. Examples of showing initiative include: – making decisions if the manager is not there – helping a colleague who is struggling to finish or understand his/her work – volunteering if a 'one-off' job needs doing for a manager
giving commitment	This means 'doing what it takes' and showing loyalty to the employer and to colleagues. Examples of commitment are: – if there is too much work to be completed in a normal working day you offer to work extra time to help out – if your employer is sponsoring a sports event to help out a local school you volunteer to go along and help
perseverance	This means 'sticking at it' and 'keeping going whatever happens'. Examples of how perseverance can help solve problems include: – if a photocopier jams and no-one can sort it out you keep trying different solutions and finally unjam it – if the cash book and the bank statement do not agree re-checking every entry until they do
embracing change	This means dealing with and making the most of change – seeing change as a challenge rather than a threat. Examples of challenges include: – accepting changes in working hours – accepting a 'sideways' move to another department which requires different work skills

Case Study

LUCINDA – USING PERSONAL SKILLS

situation

Lucinda works in the Customer Services Department of Mockingbird Ltd, an advertising business. It is 9.30am on Tuesday 5 March and the following situations arise in the office where Lucinda works.

1 Lucinda opens the following email from the Managing Director, Arthur Radley.

To: all staff
From: arthurr@mockingbird.com
Date: Tuesday, 5th March 20XX, 8.55am
Subject: Charity collection

Dear all,

As you know, the company has chosen Teenage Cancer Trust as our nominated charity to support this year. The local branch has asked us if we could provide eight volunteers to help out at the charity football match that they are organising for Saturday 9th March. It starts at 2.30pm so they need all volunteers to be there by midday. I know it's short notice but this is a really worthwhile thing to do.

Let me know by the end of Thursday 7th if you would like to help out.

Thanks and best wishes

Arthur

2 At 10.30 Lucinda needs to print out a report for her manager, Angelina, who needs it for a meeting in half an hour. She opens the file on her computer and hits the print button. Nothing happens. Lucinda walks over to the printer and sees the following message on the printer's screen:

PRINTER ERROR! PAPER JAM!

OPEN COVER AND REMOVE PAPER BEFORE CONTINUING.

Lucinda opens the printer cover but cannot remove the paper, which becomes very torn. She then gets very annoyed and flustered and reports the problem to her manager, Angelina. They discuss the situation. It seems that a number of the office's leased printers are old and keep breaking down and may need replacing. Angelina says she will get an engineer to call later in the day to ask his advice.

3 Lucinda's desk is covered with post-it notes and bits of paper with details of jobs that she needs to get done. She's beginning to feel overwhelmed by how much work she has to complete.

4 Prakash, a Marketing Manager walks over to Lucinda's desk and says: 'Hi Lucinda. I don't know if you know but Ben has recently left my team and I'm looking for a new marketing trainee. I would really like you to come and work for me. I'm afraid there wouldn't be any more money available so your salary wouldn't increase, and as you know the hours in Marketing tend to be longer than Customer Services – we're always last out of the office in the evening. This would be a great opportunity to widen your experience at Mockingbird. Have a think about it and let me know.'

5 It is the afternoon and Lucinda's Manager, Angelina, has gone for two office meetings and won't be back until at least 4.00pm. The receptionist calls at 3.00pm to say that there is a Brian Kohler in reception for Angelina. He says he is from the company that leases printers to Mockingbird Ltd and has called following a phone call from Angelina earlier in the day. Lucinda checks Angelina's diary and discovers that the visit is in the diary for 4.00pm.

TASK

Identify which of the personal skills listed on page 119 should be used to deal with these situations. Suggest the action Lucinda should take in each case.

suggested solutions

1 Lucinda should show **commitment** to her employer, Mockingbird Ltd, by volunteering to help at the charity football match.

2. Lucinda should keep calm and take time to try different ways of retrieving the torn paper. She could then get the printer working again. These actions will show **perseverance** on her part.

3. Lucinda should prioritise her tasks by considering how urgent or important each one is. This will show that she is good at **managing her time**.

4. Lucinda should seriously consider the offer that Prakash has made. It would be easy to focus on the negatives – no increase in salary and working longer hours. However, Lucinda should **embrace the change** and see the new job as a challenge and potential opportunity to progress at Mockingbird Ltd.

5. To avoid Mr Kohler having to wait an hour, Lucinda should show **initiative** by meeting with Angelina's visitor herself and discussing the issues that they have been having with the printers. However, she should take care to tell Brian Kohler that she cannot make any commitments about new printers before discussing them with Angelina.

TEAM WORKING IN THE WORKPLACE

definition

A team is a group of people working together to achieve specific objectives

A workplace team can take a number of forms, all of which will have different objectives:

- a department or 'section' working in a specific part of an office – eg a payroll section or a sales ledger section; the objective of this 'team' will be to complete the required work on time, efficiently and to a high standard
- a team set up for a specific single purpose which has a set deadline and objective, eg a planning team organising an office move
- a team set up for a specific single purpose on an ongoing basis, eg a management team within a department
- a team which draws its members from different parts of a business for a specific purpose, eg a social committee, a health and safety committee

the benefits of teamwork

People working together in a team often achieve better results than if they work on their own. The benefits include:

- **sharing skills**:
  - some people are better at some tasks and some are better at others
  - a team can take advantage of individual strengths and overcome individual weaknesses
  - team members can learn from each other
- **motivation**:
  - people get a 'buzz' out of team working and interacting with others
  - team working motivates people and brings its rewards when the team is successful
- **help and support**:
  - team members give advice and encouragement to each other
  - team members can help other team members with their work or sometimes take over tasks which may be causing a problem

things that can go wrong in a team

Dissatisfaction can cause major problems within a team. Dissatisfaction can result from:

- **management problems**:
  - the manager who does not exert enough control
  - the manager who does not communicate effectively
  - the manager who is a 'control freak' and does not allow team members to manage their own work or to show initiative
- **personal clashes**:
  - between people who have very different personalities
  - between managers and individual employees

USING SKILLS IN A TEAM

personal skills in teamwork

As you will see from the descriptions of team working on the last two pages, individual team members will need to develop personal skills so that they can become effective team players.

Personal skills enable team members to **contribute positively** to the team:

- **managing time**: this skill is important because when working in a team, team members rely on each other:
  - to keep to deadlines
  - to deal with unexpected situations
  - to be able to prioritise

  A person who can manage time reliably is an asset to any team.

- **initiative**: the qualities that this skill brings to a team include the ability to:
  - lead a discussion
  - make suggestions for future actions
  - encourage team members who seem to lack confidence by asking for their opinions and bringing them into the discussion
  - politely discourage team members who seem to have too much confidence and tend to talk over other team members

  In short, the personal skill of showing initiative means 'taking control' and is particularly appropriate to a person in a managerial position.

- **commitment**: this is the skill that involves a team member 'going the extra mile' – ie working extra hard and significantly contributing to the tasks undertaken by the team. Commitment may be shown equally by a team leader and by other team members.

- **perseverance**: this skill, which involves 'keeping going' whatever the circumstances, may be shown both by a team leader and also by other team members – although when it is shown by a team leader it also sets a good example and motivates other team members.

- **embracing (dealing with) change**: this is a personal skill which is essential to any team leader. It is important that any manager or leader must be able to deal with any change in circumstances and not panic or appear indecisive when things turn out differently to the original plan.

  Team members generally must also be willing to deal with changes to timings and to the tasks that they have been asked to carry out.

communication skills and teamwork

Communication skills are also important for people who form part of a team. As with personal skills, communication skills are **essential** for team leaders and **useful** for other team members.

Team situations require a high level of communication skills on the part of the team leader who should have a clear strategy for achieving the required objectives. This strategy should make sure that everyone agrees with the outcome and also that the main objectives are achieved.

The strategy could include any or all of the following processes:

- **leading** and directing discussions

- **resolving** disputes within the team – for example disputes over product design and development, systems for chasing bad payers, methods of marketing new products

- **negotiating** an outcome which affects the team in any way, eg hours of working, pay rates, when and where meetings are held

- **planning** improvements to existing systems and solving problems identified in the way existing systems operate

Team members who take part in team meetings and activities should be encouraged to develop their communication skills.

This process is likely to involve the way in which the team members treat other members of the team, including the team leader, and so develop '**social skills**'.

social skills – courtesy and respect for others

Employees working within a team, or at any other time when at work, should develop good **social skills** when communicating with other employees and with people outside the business. 'Good social skills' means when dealing with people, you should treat them as you would want to be treated yourself.

Social skills involve:

- **courtesy** – being polite in everyday dealings
- **respect** – showing consideration to other people
- **being helpful** – going out of your way to help others when they ask for help and also when you think they need assistance

These social skills should also extend to written communications (see Chapters 2 and 3) and telephone use (see Chapter 4) where they form the basis of 'business etiquette'.

Now read the Case Study below which shows how skills need to be used in teamwork in a business environment.

Case Study

TEAMWORK IN BUSINESS – KITTY SAVES THE DAY

situation

Mockingbird Ltd is currently in the process of moving to larger premises. The senior management team has decided to set up a largely managerial team of people – one from each department – to plan and oversee the move. The people on the committee are:

Lewis, a senior manager in the Accounts Department

Kitty, the Human Resources Manager in charge of the staffing

Oliver, a manager in the Customer Services Department

Prakash, a marketing manager

Kylie, the supervisor in the Catering Department

Everyone has gathered for the first meeting which is held on an informal basis. There are four items on the agenda:

1 Appointing a team leader

2 Timetable for the move

3 Team roles and responsibilities

4 Allocating office space

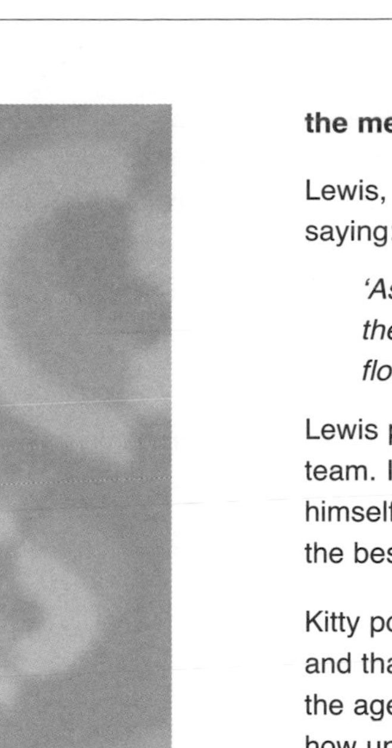

the meeting

Lewis, senior manager in the Accounts Department, starts off the discussion by saying:

> *'As I'm the only senior manager on this committee I think I should be the team leader. I have drawn up a timetable and decided on which floor each department should be allocated.'*

Lewis passes copies of the timetable and the office plan to each member of the team. It soon becomes clear that Lewis hasn't allocated any responsibilities to himself other than 'final decision making' and that the Accounts Department has the best offices in the new building.

Kitty points out that they have not agreed that Lewis should be the team leader and that the whole point of the meeting was to discuss the other three points on the agenda. Oliver and Prakash have a heated discussion with Lewis about how unfair he has been, however, Kylie does not say anything and looks very uncomfortable.

Finally, Kitty calls a halt to the discussion and calmly says:

> *'Right! We're not getting anywhere arguing about this. Let's have a sensible discussion about how we should organise this team and manage the office move. First of all we need to decide what roles and responsibilities need to be carried out. Then we can look at who has the best skills to do each of them.'*

Lewis, Oliver and Prakash stop arguing and start listening to Kitty. Kylie looks much more comfortable and nods her head enthusiastically and says in a polite tone of voice:

> *'If we are going to work effectively as a team we need to show each other some respect and consideration. We all have our own opinions but we need to make sure that we listen to what others say.'*

decisions and action points

During the meeting Lewis has eventually joined in all the discussions. By the end of the meeting he is happy with all the decisions made. These are:

- Kitty should become the team leader.
- As well as working in the Catering Department, Kylie is studying for a qualification in business administration. It has therefore been decided that she will organise all the administration for the team, including taking the minutes and drafting any communications to other staff at Mockingbird Ltd.
- Oliver will draw up a revised timetable for the move. This document will be circulated to the other four team members for approval.

- All team members should go back to their departments and discuss the allocation of office space. At the next meeting a decision will be made about the proposed new location of each department. This second meeting will also decide how the findings should be communicated to senior managers of departments not included in the original planning team.

TASK

Identify the ways in which personal skills and communication skills have been used to benefit the planning team.

solution

personal skills

- Initially Lewis has taken control of the meeting, assuming that he will be team leader. His 'control freak' attitude has resulted in a clash of personalities with Oliver and Prakash. Kitty has used her **initiative** and **perseverance** to lead and keep the discussions on track so that the problems could be resolved.
- Kylie has shown **commitment** to the business and to the team by studying for her business administration qualification and by volunteering to take on the administration for the team.
- Oliver is using his **time management** skills to draw up the timetable for the office move.
- Lewis has had to deal with the fact that Kitty will be team leader rather than him. By joining in the discussions and not bearing a grudge, Lewis has **embraced the change** so that the team can work effectively

communication skills

Kitty has taken on the role of team leader and her strong communication skills have meant that she has achieved the following:

- leading the discussions at the meeting
- resolving the dispute between Lewis, Prakash and Oliver
- encouraging Kylie to take an active role in the team
- ensuring that everyone in the team can contribute to the discussion on the allocation of office space.

Chapter Summary

- Communications in business should be made to the right person and should be correct, complete, clear and within the required timescale.
- Personal skills that are useful in business, and should be developed, include: managing time, initiative, commitment, perseverance, embracing change.
- Teamwork in business provides a number of benefits to team members: skills sharing, motivation and providing help and support.
- Examples of teams in business include departments or sections, planning teams, administrative teams and social committees.
- Communications skills used within a team are important, especially for a team leader; they include the abilities to lead discussions, sort out disputes, negotiate and plan.
- The use of social skills such as being polite and courteous, showing respect and being helpful also help a team to function effectively and to avoid internal conflict.

Key Terms

communication skills skills needed to communicate, either in writing or by word of mouth

personal skills skills which can be used and developed not only in the workplace but also in everyday life

team a group of people working together to achieve specific objectives

managing time planning ahead and dealing with unexpected events, being punctual and being able to prioritise

initiative assessing and working out what needs to be done, helping others, providing ideas and being decisive

commitment 'doing what it takes' by fully completing all tasks given, supporting colleagues and the employer

perseverance 'sticking at it' and 'keeping going whatever happens' when at work or taking exams

embracing change seeing change as a challenge rather than a threat, showing a positive attitude

8.1 Elsa is an Accounts Assistant at Spotty Dog Ltd. Her manager, Malcolm, has asked her to send an email to the other three managers in the department: Eric, Chetna, and Molly.

He tells her that she must attach the January sales spreadsheet and the agenda for the managers' meeting at 9.30am on Friday 8 October. Elsa produces the following email:

To: chetna@spottydog.com; eric@spottydog.com; polly@spottydog.com
From: elsa@spottydog.com
Date: Friday, 8 October 20XX, 9.30
Subject: Sales spreadsheet
Attachment: Decembersales.xlsx

Dear All,

Please find attached the spreadsheet that Malcolm told me to send you.

Best wishes

Elsa

Accounts Assistant

You are to identify an example of each of the following mistakes in Elsa's email and the possible problems that may result from each one. Complete the table below.

Information is sent to the wrong person
Incorrect information given
Incomplete information provided
Unclear information given
Information given when the timing is wrong

8.2 It is Wednesday morning and Betty has realised that she has too many tasks left to complete by 5.00pm on Friday (the end of the working week) when she is off on holiday for two weeks.

Decide which of the following options demonstrates that Betty is solving her problem by managing her time effectively. Select one option.

		✔
(a)	Betty emails her manager on Friday afternoon with a long list of all the jobs she has not had time to finish	
(b)	Betty writes a 'to do' list in order of priority and then emails her manager to ask if they can discuss her getting some help	
(c)	Betty selects the five hardest and most time-consuming jobs that are outstanding and gives them to her colleague to do	
(d)	Betty does all the jobs she finds straightforward and keeps her fingers crossed that no one will notice the others are outstanding until she returns	

8.3 Sheldon has been asked by his manager to check that the total of the cash in the petty cash tin agrees with the total in the petty cash book. He has tried counting the cash three times but each time it is £5 more than the total in the book.

It is now 5.00pm. He decides that he will have one final attempt at getting the totals to agree by checking all the figures in the petty cash book. This is likely to take him another half hour.

Decide which of the following combinations of personal skills Sheldon is demonstrating in this situation. Select one option.

		✔
(a)	Commitment and embracing change	
(b)	Perseverance and managing time	
(c)	Commitment and perseverance	
(d)	Initiative and embracing change	

8.4 'People working together in a team often achieve better results than if they work on their own.'

Decide whether this statement is true or false.

(a) True	
(b) False	

8.5 Bryony is a Customer Services Assistant. One of her colleagues, Zack, is constantly sending personal texts during work time. Bryony is getting very annoyed by this as it means that she and the other members of the team have to do some of his workload in order to meet deadlines. She has told her supervisor, Elspeth, about this on several occasions. Most recently, Elspeth has said to Bryony:

'I will have a think about this problem, but I suggest that to start with you need to have a quiet word with Zack and point out that private texting in working hours is annoying to others, putting them off their work and increasing the work load of others.'

The next time Zack starts texting during work time, Bryony loses her temper, shouts at him and storms out of the office.

1 Decide which one of the following options would be the best way for Elspeth to resolve this on-going problem in the Customer Services team.

		✔
(a)	Elspeth should tell Bryony to be less sensitive and to ignore Zack's texting	
(b)	Elspeth should call a team meeting to find out what the staff feel about Zack's texting	
(c)	An office policy should be put into place stating that all personal mobile phones must be left at home	
(d)	Elspeth should improve her management control over Zack's behaviour and explain to him that texting is not allowed in work time	

2 Decide what skill Bryony should develop in order to prevent her losing her temper again in the workplace. Choose one option.

		✔
(a)	commitment	
(b)	courtesy	
(c)	perseverance	
(d)	time management	

8.6 Aaron is an Accounts Assistant at Stapleford Supplies Ltd. It is 14 July and Aaron's manager, Patsy, is currently on holiday; she will not return to work until 26 July.

Aaron has just received the following email from the Sales Department:

To: aaronp@stapleford.co.uk
From: lisal@stapleford.com
Date: 14/07/20XX
Subject: sales figures

Aaron,

We are still waiting for the June sales figures which we would have expected to have received by 7 July at the latest. This is causing some serious problems, as we cannot monitor the sales of different products. If you knew you weren't going to get them done by 7 July you should have stayed late to finish them.

Some of the sales managers are getting really quite annoyed.

Please confirm we will receive the figures today.

Lisa Lebowitz

Sales Executive

Aaron is aware that there has been problems with the production of the June sales figures due to a computer system upgrade but is confident that they will be ready by 10am tomorrow morning.

(a) Should Aaron deal with this email himself or wait for Patsy to return from holiday and pass it on to her? Give reasons for your answer.

(b) Aaron is aware, from speaking to other members of the Sales Department, that Lisa Lebowitz always leaves the office at exactly 5pm and refuses to work a minute past that time. Explain whether or not you should point this out to Lisa when you next see her at the coffee machine.

Answers to activities

CHAPTER 1: COMMUNICATION SKILLS AT WORK – AN INTRODUCTION

1.1 (d) 1, 2 and 3 are all correct

1.2
1. identify the skills that you have
2. decide how good you are at these skills
3. decide which skills need improving
4. make a plan for developing your skills
5. review your progress on set target dates

1.3
(a) Emails
(d) Letters
(f) Meetings
(g) Telephone calls

1.4
(a) '**communication** skills enable you to exchange information with work colleagues and other people external to the business by word of mouth or in writing.'
(b) '**personal** skills relate to your ability to deal with people, situations and problems and will reflect your personality.'

1.5
managing time: planning ahead, dealing with unexpected events and meeting deadlines
initiative: seeing what needs to be done and then getting on and doing it
commitment: doing what it takes and showing loyalty to people and organisations
perseverance: sticking at what you have to do and keeping going whatever happens
embracing change: dealing with and making the most of change by seeing it as a challenge rather than a threat

1.6

	internal ✔	**external** ✔
A letter sent to a customer explaining that a delivery has been delayed		✔
An email sent to members of the customer services team arranging a team meeting for the following day	✔	
A directors' meeting with the business' bank manager		✔
A telephone call between the sales manager and the customer services supervisor	✔	
A telephone call between an accounts assistant and a supplier		✔
A marketing email to all customers currently on the business' database		✔

1.7 **poor business etiquette**
Martha should not have answered the phone and immediately put the caller on hold so that she could get her coffee.

suggested improvement
She should have asked who was calling and transferred the call to the appropriate person – she should have waited to collect her coffee.

---

poor business etiquette
When she returns to the call she is quite rude asking what the caller's name is despite having not previously given him a chance to speak.

suggested improvement
Martha should have said something like 'Sorry to keep you waiting, how can I help you?'

---

poor business etiquette
Martha interrupts Jeff when he is speaking.

suggested improvement
She should have let him finish what he was saying before replying.

---

poor business etiquette
'Hiya, Jeff' is too familiar when speaking to a customer and Martha talking about her personal view of his company's product is not appropriate even if it is favourable.

suggested improvement
Jeff Cummings is the Sales Director and therefore should be shown some respect. A more appropriate greeting would be 'Good morning, Mr Cummings,' or 'Good morning, Jeff' if Martha had met him previously.

---

poor business etiquette
'Hold on a sec' is too informal.

suggested improvement
Martha should have said 'If you could just hold for a moment I'll see what I can find out.'

---

poor business etiquette
Shouting across the office and not putting the call on hold is very rude, as is referring to Jeff Cummings as 'some bloke'.

suggested improvement
Martha should have put the call on hold or alternatively transferred the call to Mike, the Warehouse Manager, with a brief explanation of the issue.

CHAPTER 2: BUSINESS EMAILS

2.1 (b) false

2.2 (c) Subject: Team meeting Agenda 2.30pm 12/03/20XX

2.3 'If you use the **carbon** copy function, **all** of the recipients of the email will be able to see the other email addresses on the list.'

'If you use the **blind carbon** copy function, **none** of the recipients of the email will be able to see the other email addresses on the list.'

2.4 **You should do** the following when writing a business email: keep the email simple; be clear about what you want; use bullet points; check the grammar and spelling; keep the email thread going.

You should avoid the following when writing a business email: capital letters to emphasize a point; exclamation marks to indicate surprise; emoticons; jokes or humour; slang words.

2.5 (b) To send confidential information which is in a password-protected document.

(d) To send the arrangements for the next office team meeting to the ten members of the team.

(e) To reply to a customer email asking for the address and telephone number of your business's Customer Services Department.

(f) To place an order for more paper for the office photocopier.

2.6 (a)

- Fraser has addressed Carina as 'Dear Carina,' therefore she should have replied 'Dear Fraser' rather than the more informal 'Hi Fraser'.
- Carina has made a mistake with the order number, quoting 24478 rather than 42478.
- The first line of text includes five inappropriate exclamation marks, which Carina has used to indicate her surprise/horror.
- The question 'Is it a nice shade of blue?' is not relevant and makes it seem that Carina is not taking the issue seriously.
- The word 'notise' is spelt incorrectly and should be 'notice'.
- Despite the urgency of the situation (ie that the festival is in only four days time) Carina has said that Marcus, the Operations Manager, will contact Fraser 'sometime when he's free.'
- The word 'festivel' is spelt incorrectly and should be 'festival'.
- Carina has signed off the email with 'Have a good one!' This is not appropriate business language.

(b) Suggested email:

To: fraserbales@gosford-festivals.com
Cc: j.mcgarry@fastprint.com; m.worthington@fastprint.com
From: admin@fastprint.com
Date: Monday, 25 July 20XX, 10.30
Subject: Re: Festival T-shirts

Dear Fraser,

Order number: 42478/gosfes

Thank you for your email. I am very sorry to hear that you are unhappy with the T-shirts that you ordered from Fastprint. Our Operations Manager, Marcus Worthington, normally deals with these matters. As he is away from the office today I have forwarded your email to James McGarry, our Operations Director, who will call you later this morning to discuss the T-shirts with you.

If there is anything else I can help you with please email me.

Regards

Carina

2.7 Suggested email:

To: mauricejeffries@warmmail.com
From: elijahbanks@fabulous-footwear.com
Date: Tuesday, 07 February. 14.54
Subject: Men's shoes, Customer reference 47346MJ

Dear Mr Jeffries,

Thank you for your email regarding the men's shoes on page 24 of our new catalogue. I am very pleased that you like these shoes. If you turn to page 48 of the catalogue you will find a chart that converts European sizes to UK sizes. Alternatively, if you let me know what UK size you are I will advise you of the corresponding European size. We currently have good availability in all sizes of that style if you decide to order a pair.

Please let me know if there is anything else I can help you with.

Kind regards

Elijah Banks

CHAPTER 3: BUSINESS LETTERS

3.1

	True ✔	False ✔
An email is more formal than a business letter		✔
The language used in a letter is generally more formal that an email	✔	
A letter can often have more impact than an email	✔	
A letter takes less time to prepare than an email		✔
A letter is less commonly used than an email in a business office	✔	

3.2 (b) House style

3.3 A letter that starts 'Dear Sir' or 'Dear Madam' should end with the complimentary close 'Yours **faithfully**'

A letter that starts 'Dear Mrs Llewellyn' should end with the complimentary close 'Yours **sincerely**'

3.4

1 Printed letterhead

2 Date

3 Reference

4 Name and address of the recipient

5 Salutation

6 Subject of the letter

7 Body of the letter

8 Complimentary close

9 Signature of the sender

10 Name of the sender

11 Enclosures

3.5

Harold & Howe
Unit 5, Drayton Industrial Estate
Maynard Road
Graysville
GY14 4LG
telephone: 04164 445566
email: custserv@h&hsupplies.com

6 June 20XX

JO/ JW19327

Mr J. Wenderbury
27 Foxwell Avenue
Graysville
GY22 2PP

Dear Mr Wenderbury

Catalogue and price list request

Thank you for your letter dated 4 June and for your interest in using Howard & Howe for your building supplies. Unfortunately, we no longer provide printed catalogues and price lists to customers. However, if you visit our website www.h&hsupplies.com you will be able to download from the home page an up-to-date catalogue which includes all our prices.

If you have any problems with this please do not hesitate to contact me.

Yours sincerely

Jamie Outhwaite

J. Outhwaite
Customer Services Assistant

3.6

		True	False
(a)	The level of familiarity of the salutation (greeting) Roland uses is inappropriate	✔	
(b)	There is more than one spelling mistake in Roland's letter	✔	
(c)	It is appropriate for Roland to comment on Jenna Patel's ability to fit the conservatory doors herself as she is having problems		✔
(d)	Roland should have offered to find out who Jenna Patel spoke to himself and investigate the situation further	✔	
(e)	The complimentary close (sign off) is appropriate and matches the salutation		✔
(f)	It is acceptable to use the emoticon as Roland is signing off with his first name only		✔
(g)	Roland should have included his full name and job title below his signature	✔	

CHAPTER 4: TELEPHONES IN BUSINESS

4.1 (c) Using the same phone number to contact someone on both a landline and a mobile phone

4.2

	True	False
It is acceptable to make a personal call on the work phone line provided you are not very busy.		✔
Personal mobile phones should be kept on silent mode during office hours.	✔	
If you know the person you are contacting is busy it is more appropriate to phone them rather than send an email.		✔
It is acceptable to discuss confidential information on the phone in a large office where lots of people work.		✔
When using a telephone script it is important to stick to the precise words regardless of the answers from the customer.		✔
When travelling on a train it is better to text or email a colleague rather than having a mobile phone conversation.	✔	

4.3

1. Although Kate is self-employed, she is also a part-time employee of the health club, is on their premises and knows that she has a class starting in five minutes. She should not take the call. If it is an important call, Ryan will leave a message and Kate can then call him back after she has finished her morning at Jimmie Floyd Health Club.
2. Kate is taking a personal call in an open area of the gym. Even though the reception is bad she should not speak loudly, as this is disruptive to the other gym users and gym staff. Instead she should explain to Ryan that she will call him back after she has finished her morning at Jimmie Floyd Health Club.
3. Walking away from the class to find her diary means that Kate will be late starting the class. Once she knows what Ryan is calling about she should explain that she does not have her diary to hand and that she will call him when she has finished her morning at Jimmie Floyd Health Club to arrange a one-to-one session.
4. Despite the fact that Ryan says he is 'keen to work off some of this weight' Kate should not make a comment about how Ryan will look in his swimming trunks, and she certainly should not announce it loudly in front of a full class of people. Kate should simply have offered Ryan the slot on Tuesday afternoon and not responded specifically to his comment.
5. The phone call finishes at 10.08am, eight minutes after the class she was teaching was due to start. By taking this personal phone call she has allowed it to affect her work at the health club. She has not acted in a professional manner. As noted in (1) above, Kate should have allowed the call to go to voicemail and called Ryan back later.

CHAPTER 5: BUSINESS MEETINGS

5.1 'The **agenda** is the document that states what needs to be covered in a meeting. All items discussed at the meeting are recorded in the **minutes**. The meeting is controlled by the **chairperson** who will normally be someone senior attending the meeting. Extra items that were not originally scheduled for discussion at a meeting can be covered in **any other business**. It is important to confirm the **date and time** of the next meeting during the current meeting.

5.2 False

5.3 (d) External and formal

5.4 (a) Ishmael will be able to raise the issue under 'Any Other Business'.

(b) The team members present at the meeting should agree that the minutes of the previous month's meeting accurately reflect what was said and decided at the previous meeting. The chairperson should sign off these minutes.

(c) Ishmael's contribution to the meeting should be courteous and respectful to his fellow team members. If he uses specific examples of poor customer service this may make the individuals involved feel embarrassed or 'picked on'. He should, therefore, use general examples instead.

(d) If everyone agrees to the date and time of the next meeting at the current meeting there will be a better chance of everyone being able to attend.

5.5 (a) Errors in the previous meeting minutes may go unnoticed. There may also be action points from that meeting that will not have been actioned because no one has seen the action list.

(b) It was not sensible for Seth to nominate Sara to take the minutes of the meeting. She only recently joined the business and, as she has come straight from school, is unlikely to have taken minutes before. She has never attended a team meeting and as Seth has not provided the team with minutes of the previous meeting, Sara will not know what is normally included.

(c) An action list should have been produced as part of the minutes for the previous meeting; this lists the people who have to take action as a result of the meeting, together with a summary of what they have to do. If the minutes had been properly prepared and distributed for the previous team meeting, Michaela would have known what was expected of her.

(d) As Chairperson of the meeting, Seth is responsible for controlling what is raised in the 'Any Other Business' section of the meeting. He should have politely but firmly stopped Arthur and explained that the Accounts Department departmental meeting was not the appropriate forum for this matter and he would be better raising it with the Catering Manager.

CHAPTER 6: PERSONAL SKILLS AT WORK

6.1 (b) The urgency and importance of the tasks

6.2 (a) Volunteering to produce the report

(d) Including the additional information about customers who unsubscribed

6.3 (b) Volunteer to stay late yourself and produce the report

6.4 (c) Having tried to find the difference she re-inputs the balances, checking each one thoroughly before moving onto the next

6.5 The following **are** embracing change:

(a) 'That's good as I won't have to come back to the office after work on a Friday to get my time sheet authorised'

(c) 'It would be a really good idea if the system could show us a summary of the work we've done so we can check that we agree with it'

(e) 'This will mean that we have proof of how many hours we've been at a job if they query the bill'

(f) 'It might take a bit of getting used to but at least I don't have to rely on my memory when I'm completing my timesheet at the end of the week'

The following are **not** embracing change:

(b) 'Is this just another way of reducing how much we get paid?'

(d) 'Sounds like Big Brother will be watching us!'

CHAPTER 7: EVALUATING SKILLS

7.1 'When thinking about what job to apply for you should first carry out a **skills analysis** to identify your **strengths** and **weaknesses**'

7.2 'A **job description** sets out the job title, the tasks that have to be done and the responsibilities of the job.'

'A **person specification** lists the skills, experience and qualifications that an individual needs for carrying out the job.'

7.3 Goals that are set at a job appraisal can be short-term goals or long-term goals. Short-term goals are those that you plan to achieve in up to **one** year and long-term goals are those that you plan to achieve in up to **five** years.

7.4

S	Specific
M	Measurable
A	Achievable
R	Realistic
T	Time bound

7.5

Manager:	'The project must be completed by the end of September.'
SMART objective	**Time bound**
Manager:	'You can allocate one day per week to complete this project.'
SMART objective	**Achievable**
Val:	'I'm really going to work hard to get this database up and running.'
SMART objective	**Realistic**
Manager:	'I have set up a standard template for each customer for you to use. All 400 customers need to be added to the database.'
SMART objective	**Specific**
Val:	'Once I have completed the database I will get my supervisor, Jill, to test it to make sure it meets the department's needs.'
SMART objective	**Measurable**

7.6

	Efficient	Effective
Producing the result that you have planned for.		✔
Getting the job done with the minimum waste of effort and resources.	✔	

7.7

	Formal	Informal
A work colleague says the spreadsheet you have produced is very useful.		✔
At your annual job appraisal your manager says that he is very pleased with the new filing system you have organised and set up.	✔	
Your tutor tells you in class that your class attendance is unacceptable and that you need to improve this in order to pass your course.		✔
Your classmate tells you that you have got the double-entry question you are doing in class wrong.		✔

CHAPTER 8: PROBLEM SOLVING AND TEAM WORKING

8.1 **Information is sent to the wrong person**

Elsa has sent the email to polly@spottydog.com rather than molly@spottydog.com.

Result: This could result in the wrong person getting the Sales spreadsheet and Molly not having the correct information for the meeting.

Incorrect information given

Elsa has sent the December sales spreadsheet rather than the one for January.

Result: This means that the managers will not have the correct information for the meeting on Friday.

Incomplete information provided

Malcolm has asked Elsa to send the agenda and the spreadsheet for the meeting, however she has only sent the (wrong) spreadsheet.

Result: The managers will not know what is on the agenda for the meeting on Friday and may not be fully prepared for it.

Unclear information given

Elsa's email is very brief and does not explain which sales spreadsheet is attached or the fact that there is a meeting on Friday morning.

Result: The managers may not look at the spreadsheet and may not realise that there is a meeting on Friday.

Information given when the timing is wrong

Elsa has sent the email at exactly the time the meeting is due to start.

Result: The managers will not have the necessary information for the Friday morning meeting and it may have to be rearranged.

8.2 (b) Betty writes a 'to do' list in order of priority and then emails her manager to ask if they can discuss her getting some help.

8.3 (c) Commitment and perseverance

8.4 True

8.5 1 (d) Elspeth should improve her management control over Zack's behaviour and explain to him that texting is not allowed in work time

2 (b) courtesy

8.6 (a) Aaron should deal with this matter himself. The email is addressed to him and he has all the necessary information to inform Lisa Lebowitz when the Sales Department will receive the figures. This matter can be resolved quickly and efficiently rather than waiting until Patsy returns from her holiday.

(b) Aaron should not bring up this matter with Lisa Lebowitz. It is not his job to do this and it would be discourteous to criticise another employee at the coffee machine when other members of staff might hear.

Index

for your notes

for your notes

for your notes

for your notes